1915 CAMPAIGN IN FRANCE
THE BATTLES OF AUBERS RIDGE FESTUBERT AND LOOS
Considered in relation to the Field Service Regulations

1915 CAMPAIGN IN FRANCE
THE BATTLES OF AUBERS RIDGE, FESTUBERT & LOOS
Considered in relation to the Field Service Regulations

These notes and sketches have been compiled from official sources and from information received from those who took part in the battles.

BY

A. KEARSEY, D.S.O., O.B.E., p.s.c.
LATE LIEUTENANT-COLONEL, GENERAL STAFF

SECOND EDITION

PRINTED AND BOUND
IN GREAT BRITAIN BY
ANTONY ROWE LTD, EASTBOURNE

CONTENTS

INTRODUCTION vii

CHAPTER		PAGE
I.	APPRECIATION OF THE SITUATION BEFORE THE BATTLE OF AUBERS RIDGE	1
	APPRECIATION OF THE SITUATION BEFORE THE BATTLE OF FESTUBERT	9
	APPRECIATION OF THE SITUATION BEFORE THE BATTLE OF LOOS	14
II.	BATTLE OF AUBERS RIDGE (ILLUSTRATING F.S.R.) ...	27
III.	BATTLE OF FESTUBERT (ILLUSTRATING F.S.R.) ...	32
IV.	BATTLE OF LOOS (ILLUSTRATING F.S.R.)	39
V.	DIARY OF EVENTS	63

Four sketches compiled from official maps by kind permission of His Majesty's Stationery Office.

BATTLE OF AUBERS RIDGE, MAY 9TH, 1915	91
BATTLE OF FESTUBERT, MAY 15TH–25TH, 1915	92
GENERAL SITUATION, SEPTEMBER 25TH, 1915	93
BATTLE OF LOOS, SEPTEMBER 25TH–OCTOBER 8TH, 1915	94

INDEX 95

PRESS OPINIONS.

"*Cavalry Journal,*" October, 1929.

"1915 CAMPAIGN IN FRANCE" comprises appreciations of the situation at various dates, diaries of events, and narratives of battles, with copious references to F.S.R. A number of simple sketch maps facilitate the comprehension of the operation dealt with."

"*Fighting Forces,*" October, 1929.

"This book should prove of unquestioned value and real interest to Army officers. The author has succeeded admirably in his aim. We can strongly recommend this useful little book."

INTRODUCTION.

It is hoped that this unofficial work, compiled from official despatches and from notes received from those who took part in the actions, may prove helpful to those who have not had the time for extensive research, and who consequently may be glad to have the main points presented to them in a concise form.

This work is the result of a very great deal of study and also of personal experience on the Western Front. The author's endeavour has been to make comments with judgment and impartiality.

These lines, written by Charles Nodier, appear to apply to the situations in this book, as they ring with a gay challenge, bidding us surmount the peace and war difficulties, which we had to deal with in the preparation for the 1914 campaign and in the 1915 battles:—

> Que Dieu daigne vous donner à tous
> Mes bons amis
> Tout ce qu'il faut de patience
> Pour supporter la vie,
> D'amour et de bienveillance,
> Pour la rendre douce et utile,
> Et de gaieté
> Pour s'en moquer.

These difficulties are described in Volume IV, Military Operations, with a sympathy that makes the volume most interesting reading, and with a candour that makes it most instructive. Very clearly the author brings out the point that the limited results obtained at Festubert and Loos were due to our inexperienced and partly trained troops having the severe handicap of less heavy guns, bombs, trench warfare equipment and material than the enemy opposed to them. It is also shown how we had to defer to the wishes of the French G.Q.C. to carry out offensive operations in difficult country and under unfavourable tactical conditions.

The reasons for our failure at Fromelles and Rue de Bois on May 9th and for the more encouraging results at Festubert between May 15th and 25th are clearly brought out. One main reason appears to have been that we had to postpone our offensive operations after the Neuve Chapelle battle, and that then until May 9th the Germans turned their light field defences into semi-permanent fortifications. We had not a sufficient quantity of effective heavy H.E. shell to destroy them.

Then, in the account of the Battle of Loos, the author points out that we based our plan on the possibilities attainable by the use of gas, and that, though this failed on some parts of the line, a considerable success was achieved, but it was not exploited adequately, as the 21st and 24th Divisions in general reserve were too far back and the delay in assigning them definitely to the First Army caused the favourable moment for their employment to be lost. In addition, the Germans, since the commencement of our offensive at the Battle of Aubers Ridge, had constructed a stronger second line than the one which we had been unable to capture on May 9th. This line was protected by a thick belt of wire, and it was out of range from our trenches. Only near Cité St. Elie and in front of Haisnes were any parts of it captured, and these could not be maintained.

Further instructive comments are made on the renewal of frontal assaults at places where there had been a repulse when outflanking movements would have been more effective. The difficulties of maintaining direction in the attack, of arranging for the collection and transmission of information, of leadership and of staff work in new commands are clearly shown.

This is only a summary of what readers will find poignantly interesting in Volume IV, Military Operations.

1915 CAMPAIGN IN FRANCE.

CHAPTER I.

APPRECIATION OF THE SITUATION BEFORE THE BATTLE OF AUBERS RIDGE, FOUGHT ON MAY 9TH, 1915.

GENERAL SITUATION.—From April 22nd, 1915, the Second Battle of Ypres was being fought, and it was continued until the result of our offensive operations were felt by the Germans in the vicinity of Festubert.

In this second Ypres battle we were able to hold a salient round Ypres, but we suffered heavily from the enemy's poisoned gas and from their superior numbers of high explosive shell and machine guns; but they gained no special advantage in their position.

The result of the battle was that a more effective policy was being demanded by the public for the supply of war material. Our heavy casualties at the battle of Ypres it was thought were the result of insufficient preparation and forethought. The urgent need for ammunition had not been foreseen, and indeed it would have been difficult for our Defence Committee to have visualized the necessity for such a vast expenditure.

There was a growing demand for organization on economical and scientific lines for war. Our peace organization was not suited to deal with the war machine of a powerful industrial people who concentrated on what they considered would enable them to fulfil their ambitions.

They still were able to get their supplies from neutral countries, as we had not turned to account our great advantage of sea power in making a complete blockade. Our strength in war consists in our power and right to prevent our enemies from obtaining sea supplies while we and our friends do receive them.

The military importance of sea communications and sea transport was not yet realized, and that by not exercising our rights on the sea we were prolonging the war. We did not apparently consider that when nations are fighting on land all available power should be used to shorten and win a war.

The heavy transport of the world is still carried on the surface of the sea, so the sea communications are consequently vulnerable, and if controlled by the British Navy will be the point at which Great Britain can strike a decisive blow against her enemies.

This blow we withheld for some time, and in consequence the war was protracted, and we had to suffer on land from the new devices of poison gas, which the enemy were able to construct from material received from across the communications which we could have dominated.

War must be a choice of evils, and it is said that our complete blockade would cause suffering to innocent civilians, but it would have been more merciful to all concerned had we shortened the war by early drastic action which we could have justly taken, instead of allowing it to be prolonged and consequently adding to the casualties of the civilians, who had to be trained for war and brought into the trenches.

Our heavy casualty list included all sections of the community taken from their work in civil life to face the modern inventions of the German mechanics and scientists. We had at hand a powerful weapon, which was more certain than any other, and though by using our sea power we might have made the civilians of hostile nations hungry, yet we should have been able to accomplish the object of our declaration of war without the loss of life and destruction entailed by protracting it for four years and three months. It must be the basis of all our war policy that we maintain at all costs an effective control of the surface of the sea.

This problem, with the supply of ammunition and with the adapting of our economic system to the changing situation at home and in Europe, it was felt by the public, were not being completely realized by those responsible for the conduct of operations.

The Germans had foreseen the necessity for heavy and mobile artillery supplied with great quantities of high explosive ammunition. Their organization included all their military and industrial resources, and they had evolved plans to make full use of all their power.

On the other hand the general feeling was that we were inclined to carry out the policy that had been evolved in past wars, and that our men in contact with the enemy were suffering owing to lack of preparation and prevision. In war, if there is lack of forethought and insight there will be heavy casualties, just as in the economical world, if there is a lack of thought and adaptability, there will be loss of money.

Our casualties had been very heavy. The leading of the troops in the actual operations had been beyond reproach, but there was a growing feeling that every endeavour should be made to co-operate all the resources of the nation to save unnecessary loss in the field and to give the troops at least an equal chance with gases, shells, bullets, and grenades in the fight with Germany.

A system it was now seen was required for dealing with this war. Our previous system of party politics had enabled men to reach lucrative positions if they cultivated powers of argument and fluency of speech, but the present crisis required men of administrative ability, who could look beyond the triumph in debate to the solution of important and difficult problems, which would enable us to save life and to shorten the war.

We had realized from the Battle of Neuve Chapelle the necessity of high explosive shells and the great efforts made by Germany to obtain them for the protection of her 1,400 miles of front in Europe and for the reinforcement of Turkey. We had more than a million men training in England; the French, too, had new armies ready and her ammunition supply had been enormously increased.

The German position outside Europe was not too satisfactory.

The Japanese had captured her Asiatic possession—Tsingtau. Her Pacific possessions had been taken from her. General Botha had overrun German South-West Africa. The important parts of the Cameroons had been captured. Togoland was now in our hands. There was complete unity of purpose among the Allies, who had agreed to make definite peace together on terms to which all agreed, nor was there any relaxation of effort among any of the people of the countries engaged in the war. There was a strong feeling, which the heavy casualties at the Battle of Ypres did much to foster, that the effort and resolution of the nation must be backed up by a governing body that was not only efficient, but, in addition, able to think ahead and to anticipate requirements. In the Balkans, Germany had not gained the advantages hoped for from her victories in Galicia and Poland.

Bulgaria had not yet joined the German Alliance. Rumania and Greece were still neutral.

During April the French had made progress in Alsace, on both banks of the River Fecht and by capturing the height of Les Eparges. Now their plan was to relieve the pressure on Russia by striking as strongly as possible at a point on the Western Front which threatened seriously the Germans' communications and the stability of their front line.

This point was in Artois. An advance towards Douai over the plain of the River Scheldt would strike at the German communications of their three armies on a 100-mile front between Reims and Lille at a time when the total numbers of the Germans on the Western Front were half a million less than those of the Allies.

1. OBJECT. The object of the Allies on the Western Front was to help the Russians, against whom the Germans were preparing to strike with all their available reserves between Gorlice and Tarnow. The numbers of Germans on the Eastern Front were to be increased by approximately 100,000 men for their sixty-four divisions on this front.

The British First Army was to co-operate by taking the offensive with the French Tenth Army towards Douai and Aubers Ridge.

2. FACTORS affecting its attainment:

(a) *Strength and location of opposing forces.* Our First Army consisted of the I Corps, containing the 1st, 2nd, and 47th Divisions; the IV Corps, with the 7th, 8th, and 49th Divisions; and the Indian Corps, containing the 51st, Lahore, and Meerut Divisions. In Army Reserve were five cavalry divisions, the Canadian, 50th and 51st Divisions.

Attached to the First Army were three squadrons of the Royal Flying Corps. On our front the Germans had the 6th Bavarian Reserve Division, and VII Corps consisting of the 13th and 14th Divisions. In Army Reserve on our front they had the 58th Division at Roubaix and the 115th at Tournai.

Farther south, on the front of the French Tenth Army, the Germans had six divisions from their XIV Corps near Lens; their 1st Bavarian Regiment was near Vimy and their IV Corps was south of Bailleul. The French Tenth Army, on the front of over twenty miles from south of Vermelles to north of Arras, was held by their IX, XXI, XXXIII, XX, XVII and X Corps.

On the front of attack the Allies had a superiority in numbers, but in view of the strength of the German trenches and wire obstacles our artillery and our ammunition supply were insufficient, so that our preliminary bombardment of the German defences could only be carried out for forty minutes, of which only ten minutes could be intensive, before our first attack on May 9th.

The French considered that their lack of success was due to shortage of artillery and ammunition, although before their attack, starting at 1000 hours on May 9th, they bombarded the enemy's trenches for six days with 1,252 guns.

As to location, the Germans in our front held a salient, of which La Bassée was the point, surrounded by brickfields, mines and enclosures, all strongly fortified. Throughout their defences they had a number of fortresses manned by machine gunners and joined by a series of fire and communication trenches, from which they could bring both frontal and enfilade fire to bear on an enemy advancing from the west. Therefore a direct attack on it must have been slow and costly.

An advance, however, from the River Lys, south of Armentières, to the ridge four miles west of Lille which runs south-west to Aubers, two miles east of Neuve Chapelle, ending on the Haut Pommereau Hill and from this position on to another ridge which follows the road from Lille through Fournes to La Bassée, would enable us to turn the German position at La Bassée and would cause them to evacuate it and the ground in its vicinity.

Since the Battle of Neuve Chapelle, in March, 1915, the Germans had been improving their lines between Lille and La Bassée. The trenches were deep and wide and were reinforced by concrete dug-outs to shelter the garrisons. Their barbed wire fences had been strengthened and thickened. Their ammunition reserves had been increased and their heavy guns at Pont à Vendin, five and a half miles south-east of La Bassée, were well posted to deal with troops advancing on this town.

South of the hill on which La Bassée stood was a plain covered by factory chimneys and slag-heaps. North of La Bassée to Neuve Chapelle the country was low-lying and water-logged, and intersected with broad ditches filled with mud and water and hidden by long grass. A few clumps of trees gave cover for the enemy's machine guns.

The country round Lens is flat. South of this town runs a ridge on which stands Notre Dame de Lorette. In the valley south of this town is Ablain St. Nazaire, east of which is Carency in a low-lying plain, in which stands the Bois de Berthonvale dominated by Mont St. Eloi.

East of Carency the ground rises to the low hills of Vimy Ridge, which commands the communications between Arras and Lens. On the eastern side of Vimy Ridge the ground falls gradually to the Plain of Douai.

(b) *Morale and Training.* The Germans, in strong entrenchments defended by numerous machine guns and covered by wire entanglements, were a formidable enemy. Our casualties had been so heavy that the original Army had been considerably diminished and the New Armies were not expected to be ready to take the offensive against a well-armed and prepared enemy. The Commander-in-Chief would have preferred to wait until staff officers and unit commanders could be more adequately trained and until we had sufficient material and technical equipment.

The Germans remedied any defects in their depleted Army by adding a mass of artillery, strengthened trenches, and mechanical devices to support the troops holding the lines which they wanted to maintain until the Russians had been defeated by von Mackensen's Army.

(c) *Communications.* By means of our combined offensive with the French Tenth Army towards Douai and Aubers Ridge, we should be in a position to dominate the enemy's most direct communications between Lille and Cambrai and subsequently against the railways in the gap between the Ardennes and Holland.

The attacks of the French Fourth Army in Champagne between Ville-sur-Tourne and Auberive, if successful, and pressed forward towards the Rhine crossings, would cut the communications between Mezières and Laon. Our further advance would cut the line between Valenciennes and Brussels. The whole of the operations now were directed against the German communications.

(d) *Supplies.* Our means of supply were vastly superior to those of the enemy, owing to our sea power. The German Fleet remained inactive behind the Frisian Islands, and the Austrian Fleet was in the north-east corner of the Adriatic. Their raid on the coast on January 24th had been defeated, as had also been Von Spee's fleet at the Battle of the Falkland Islands. Their submarine campaign had led them into hostility with neutral nations, and had only disabled less than 1½ per cent. of our total shipping. We were able to maintain our campaign in the Dardanelles and in East Africa, and to keep open our communications with Australia, New Zealand, India, and Egypt.

(e) *Time and Space.* From the starting lines of our main attacks on May 9th to our first objectives between Rue du Marais and Fromelles, the distance was approximately two miles, and it was five miles farther east to our second objectives on the Haute Deule Canal at Bauvin and Don. Our IV Corps was on a 5,000-yard front facing German trenches held by three regiments. The I and Indian Corps were on a front of 8,500 yards between Givenchy and Neuve Chapelle, facing German trenches held by four regiments.

Our attacks were to be converging towards Aubers, and they were to join up on the inner flanks of the IV and Indian Corps at La Cliqueterie Farm, 1,500 yards south of Aubers.

The direction of our advance towards Aubers was to be from the north-west by the IV Corps, and from the southwest respectively by the I and Indian Corps. Our attack from the north-west was to be through Rouges Bancs, 2,200 yards north-east of Aubers, towards this village, which was 3,000 yards east of our front line. The German front line was approximately 100 to 200 yards away from our forward trenches.

There was a further gap of fifteen miles between our offensive towards Aubers and the French attacks towards Vimy. Their front of attack was approximately nine miles from south of Roclincourt to the north of Notre Dame de Lorette. From the centre of their line to the top of Vimy Ridge was two and a half miles. The nearest Army reserves available to exploit success on the front of the Tenth Army were seven and a half miles west of their front line. The two German reserve divisions east of their line on our front were at Roubaix and Tournai, eighteen and twenty-five miles north-east and east respectively of Neuve Chapelle. They were able to leave these places and reach positions south of Lens in four hours.

The time was chosen for the combined offensive with the French Tenth Army to take advantage of the weakening on the Western Front of the German forces for their assault with the Austrians against the Russians, commencing on May 1st, 1915, in their attempt to drive the Russians out of Galicia and Poland. Our offensive operations were also undertaken to encourage Italy to join the Allies.

3. COURSES:

Open to the Allies were to remain in their present positions until adequate numbers of staff and regimental officers had been trained, and until artillery and ammunition were sufficient to demolish the strong German works in our front and to support adequately our attacking troops. This course would have been acting entirely in our interests, without regard to our Russian Allies. For the British Army it would have been specially advantageous to wait until our New Armies were more fully trained.

Our casualties were, as stated in the Official History, Vol. IV, often due to loss of direction and failure to keep communication, and to the fact that, owing to the inferior quality of the ammunition, " British gunners were unable to hit their targets and the German counter-batteries and machine guns were not silenced."

However, in order to afford relief to our Allies, our offensive operations had to be carried out as early as possible in co-operation with the French Tenth Army, who were holding the line immediately south of our First Army.

The courses open to the Germans on our front were limited to the occupation of their positions, as they were still fighting the Second Battle of Ypres, which they began on April 22nd, and the rest of their troops available for offensive action had started their battles against the Russians on May 1st.

Their only troops available for independent action were the 58th Division at Roubaix and the 115th Division at Tournai. They could make use of them to strengthen the local reserves on their front between Rouges Bancs and Rue du Marais, or between Loos and Bailleul. Their policy after they had failed to gain their objective in mobile warfare was to economize strength by adding to their fortifications and to supplement their local weakness at any point by increased artillery support.

For this support, they made full use of all their national resources to amass quantities of shells for their guns of all calibres. In order, therefore, to take advantage of the comparative numerical weakness of the Germans on our front, the following plan was adopted.

Plan. Our plan was to start offensive operations on our front on May 9th with a bombardment of the enemy's forward defences, guns and wire at 0500 hours. At 0530 hours, this bombardment was to become intensive for ten minutes, and was then to lift 600 yards. At 0540 hours, the infantry assault was to start simultaneously on the front held by the I, Indian and IV Corps. The French Tenth Army was to start their attack at 1000 hours. Our I and Indian Corps were to attack from the south of Neuve Chapelle. The IV Corps were to attack from the vicinity of Rouges Bancs. The general direction of all the Corps was Aubers Ridge.

The general objective for the First Army was first the La Bassée-Fournes Road, three miles from our front trenches, and then another four miles to the Haute Deule Canal, including the villages of Bauvin and Don, two and a half miles apart.

The first general objective for the French Tenth Army was the capture of Vimy Ridge and the ground between Farbus and Souchez, approximately four and a half miles apart and two and a half miles from their front lines.

North of this main attack, their XXI Corps was to capture the Notre Dame de Lorette Ridge, and south of it their XVII Corps was to advance north-east on either side of Ecurie.

The details of our plan were that the 1st Division and the Meerut Division together on a 2,400-yard front at 0540 hours were to advance in an easterly direction from the south of Neuve Chapelle, and the 8th Division on a 1,500-yard front was to advance at 0540 hours towards Fromelles.

The result of this Battle of Aubers Ridge by the evening of May 9th was that in places we gained a footing in the German front-line trenches. Our numbers, however, owing to heavy losses, were insufficient first to exploit success, and later to maintain it. Our limited ammunition supply was neither effective nor sufficient to support our further attacks, as the enemy's trenches and wire had been found to be stronger than was expected. The regiments of the German Sixth Army opposing our attacks were thus able to hold their positions without the help of their two reserve divisions, which during this day were sent to reinforce their IX Corps and 1st Bavarian Regiment in front of the French fighting in the vicinity of Vimy.

APPRECIATION OF THE SITUATION BEFORE THE BATTLE OF FESTUBERT, WHICH WAS STARTED ON MAY 15TH, AND WAS CONTINUED UNTIL MAY 25TH, 1915.

GENERAL SITUATION. The Italians had rejected their obligations under the Triple Alliance. By sinking the unarmed passenger steamer, the *Lusitania*, the Germans lost the sympathy of the civilized world.

General Foch was determined to continue the offensive on the front of the French Tenth Army, in order to gain Vimy Ridge, the occupation of which would facilitate our progress across the Plain of Lens and Douai. Our Second Army was still fighting hard in the Ypres Salient.

Our high-explosive ammunition supply was not as plentiful as it should be for the destruction of the very strong wire and defences which the Germans were daily strengthening. Our ammunition shortage was accentuated by the necessity of sending shells to the Dardanelles, where our operations at the Second Battle of Krithia had not led to the successful results that had been expected. This was serious, as the short bombardment before our assault on May 9th had not been a complete success, and it was hoped to make a long, intensive bombardment to breach the German trenches and to cut paths through their wire.

The German successes in Galicia had made us apprehensive as to the possibility of the invasion of England, so that the New Army would not be available for our offensive operations at Festubert.

However, it was resolved to co-operate actively with the French, who were making every effort to defeat the Germans, whose forces in the West were depleted while they were involved in a struggle with Russia.

1. OBJECT. Our object was to break through the German forward defences, to press on towards Violaines and Beau Puits, and thus to assist the operations of the French Tenth

Army in the capture of Vimy Ridge, and to maintain such pressure on the enemy in our front that they could not send reinforcements to strengthen their opposition to the French attacks against the Labyrinth, Neuville St. Vaast, and Souchez.

2. FACTORS affecting its attainment.

(a) *Strength and Location of Opposing Forces.* Our available forces for our first offensive operations were the 47th, 7th, 2nd, Lahore, and Meerut Divisions. The Canadian Division (less artillery) was the I Corps reserve; the Indian Cavalry Corps and 51st Division were in Army reserve.

On our immediate front, the German VII Corps Commander for our initial attacks had the 55th and 15th Regiments holding the front opposite our 2nd Division and Indian Corps, and the 5th Regiment opposite our 7th Division. Therefore, we had a numerical superiority on the front of attack. The Germans had suffered heavy casualties, and they had only local reserves in the vicinity of their forward positions. The German positions, however, were very strong, and their machine guns were numerous and concealed. The country was flat and the trees were in leaf, so that it was very difficult to locate the enemy's guns and machine guns, and to observe our artillery fire.

Their forward trenches were protected by thick wire entanglements, the front of which was under their close and effective fire. The waterlogged fields intersected with deep, muddy trenches added to the difficulties of our advancing troops. The Germans, owing to the strength of their position, and owing to our lack of the best kind of high-explosive ammunition suited to destroying them, had an advantage and were able to economize men on their Western, while they took all their available reserves to their Russian, Front.

(b) *Morale, Training and Armament.* There was in England a growing feeling of the necessity of taking steps to grapple with the rearrangement of industry and social life, and of making a Coalition Ministry. The Secretary of State for War pointed out in the House of Lords that, unless the whole nation co-operated, not only in supplying the manhood of the country to serve in our ranks, but also in supplying the necessary arms, ammunition and equipment, successful operations in the various parts of the world in which we were engaged would be seriously hampered and delayed. He went on to state: " We have unfortunately found that the output is not only not equal to our necessities, but does not fulfil our expectations—it is absolutely essential not only that the arrears

1915 CAMPAIGN IN FRANCE

in the deliveries of our munitions of war should be wiped off, but that the output of every round of ammunition is of the utmost importance and has a large influence on our operations in the field."

In addition to our inadequate supply of H.E. and gas ammunition, our armament was not sufficient. Many of the New Army divisions had not got their complement of guns and we could not distribute half as many guns per mile of front as the French could. For our continuous sixty hours' bombardment on May 13th, 14th and 15th, we had 121 howitzers, varying from fifty-four 4.5 inch to two 15-inch howitzers. We had also 312 guns varying from four 6-inch to sixteen 15-pounders.

Much of the ammunition, however, was faulty, and, owing to the wet, misty weather, observation of fire was difficult; nor could the explosion of the bulk of the H.E. shells be seen, owing to the sodden condition of the ground on May 13th and 14th.

As to the training of our troops, there was still a shortage of experienced leaders and of trained staff officers, so that, if it had been possible to postpone further operations, it would have been to our advantage.

(c) *Time and Space.* The distance to our first objectives on La Quinque Rue was approximately 1,000 yards from our front-line trenches. Our three brigades attacking in a south-easterly direction between Chocolat Menier Corner and Port Arthur were on a frontage of 2,000 yards.

The 7th Division was to attack, on a two-brigade frontage of 425 yards for each brigade, in an easterly direction from the north of Festubert. There were 600 yards between the inner flanks of the two attacking divisions, namely, the 2nd and 7th.

The distance between Festubert and Port Arthur was 5,000 yards. It was on this frontage that the enemy's trenches were to be bombarded. The distance to our second objective, the line Rue d'Ouvert-Rue du Marais, was 2,000 yards from our front line. To the centre of our third objective at Violaines between Chapelle St. Roch and Beau Puits it was 3,000 yards from our forward trenches.

3. COURSES open to the First Army.

(a) To remain in their present positions and wait for a more favourable opportunity to undertake offensive operations, that is, when we had adequate reserves of trained leaders and men, and ample supplies of H.E. shells and gas. This would have saved us very many casualties, but it would not have been in accordance with the general plan which the

French wished to carry out, and for which they thought that the opportunity was favourable.

(*b*) To continue the offensive with all available troops, in order to help the French and the Russians.

The Russians were being driven back, and it was necessary to make a diversion in their favour to prevent more troops being sent against them. This might not have been possible had we remained inactive.

The French wished to take advantage of the comparative weakness of the Germans on the Western Front to make a big effort as early as possible, to drive them out of France by simultaneous offensive operations from Verdun and Nancy; from Reims in a north-easterly direction; and in an easterly direction from Artois.

The French expected and asked for active co-operation from the British on the northern flank of their Tenth Army. In spite of our commitments in the Dardanelles, our difficult position in the Ypres Salient, where there was stiff fighting, and in spite of the considered necessity of keeping troops in England, it was decided to make every effort to help the French by attacking on our front from north of Festubert to one and a quarter miles south of Neuve Chapelle, in order to break through the German defences up to a line between Chapelle St. Roch and Beau Puits, and so to prevent the Germans from sending troops from our front to reinforce the points where the French were pressing their attacks.

Such an opportunity for offensive action might not occur again.

To the French, the request for our active co-operation was naturally reasonable enough, as they were, of course, anxious to rid their country of the burden of the German occupation, and they might consider that after nearly ten months of war we might have the men and material ready to help them on this front.

The courses open to the Germans were, in view of their comparative numerical weakness, to strengthen their trenches, machine-gun emplacements and wire as much as possible, and to add to their ammunition supplies, in order to be ready for an attack, until their policy on their Eastern Front had been successfully carried out.

They could then, with superior numbers, hope to take the offensive on their Western Front. This was the course which they were pursuing.

Their trench lines were strong, their wire entanglements were thick, their machine-gun emplacements were concealed, and their ammunition supplies, heavy howitzers, machine guns and stick grenades were adequate.

1915 CAMPAIGN IN FRANCE

They had, as soon as they had failed to gain their objectives after the Battle of the Marne, realized that the form of war, which was being forced on both combatants as their flanks were being spread out to the sea, would require stores of ammunition. They had devoted all the national resources to build up the necessary types of shells, while their scientists and chemists had evolved a method of spreading death with gas generators over a larger surface than was possible with the contents of the largest shell.

4. PLAN. The French plan, in which we were to cooperate, therefore, was to act as early as possible in dealing vigorously with the enemy in our front before their lines became stronger and before their troops returned from their Eastern Front.

While the French Army continued to attack towards Souchez and Neuville St. Vaast, the plan for the First Army was to renew the offensive north of Festubert with a deliberate and persistent attack, starting on May 15th after a methodical bombardment.

South of Festubert, for a front of two and a quarter miles, the 47th and 1st Divisions were to hold the line. The 1st Division was to take over the line from the French 58th Division. The details of the plan were for the assault to start at 2330 hours on the night of May 15th/16th after the preliminary bombardment of thirty-six hours had been continued for sixty hours.

This first assault was to be carried out by three brigades, namely, the 6th and 5th from the 2nd Division on a front of 1,300 yards, supported by the Garhwal Brigade from the Meerut Division on a front of 400 yards. On reaching their first objective on La Quinque Rue, they were to join up with the 7th Division, who were to start their attack at dawn, and who were to continue the advance in an easterly direction up to the vicinity of Chapelle St. Roche-Beau Puits.

The Royal Flying Corps were to co-operate by bombing the German VII Corps and 14th Division's headquarters, their observation posts, and the railways running to Lille. The 7th Division was to attack at dawn on May 16th, with the 22nd and 20th Brigades, on a front of 850 yards. The southern flank of the 7th Division was to be protected by the 47th Division, and the northern flank of the Garhwal Brigade by the remainder of the Meerut Division.

During the days and nights up to May 25th, when our offensive operations were concluded, in spite of heavy casualties, owing to our shortage of ammunition and grenades and our small number of guns as compared with the Germans, ground was won on a front of four miles to an average depth of 600 yards.

On May 15th, the French Tenth Army made three definite attempts to break through to their objectives, and they were able to capture some trenches in the Labyrinth and some houses in the western end of Neuville St. Vaast.

Three weeks later they renewed their attacks in these two areas with success. On June 18th, they brought their offensive operations to a conclusion.

APPRECIATION OF THE SITUATION BEFORE THE BATTLE OF LOOS, WHICH STARTED ON SEPTEMBER 25TH AND WAS CONTINUED UNTIL OCTOBER 8TH, 1915.

SITUATION. The British Armies in France had now been reinforced and had been able to extend their right wing to Grenay, west of Lens, from south of Boesinghe, which is three and a half miles north of Ypres.

The boundary between our Second and First Armies was a north-westerly line running south of Armentières and striking our forward trenches two miles south-east of this town. The French, too, had been reinforced. Nine new divisions had been formed by amalgamation and by reductions of the strength of companies.

The salient position which the Germans occupied between Verdun, Reims, Soissons, Noyon, Albert, Arras, and Ypres encouraged the idea that an offensive operation in a northerly direction from Champagne and in an easterly direction from Artois would cut off the twenty-three German divisions of their Seventh, First and Second Armies in the point of their salient in Picardy.

The situation, however, for the British was complicated, as our final offensive from Suvla Bay in Gallipoli had failed, and our Commander there required reinforcements, so that it would have suited us to postpone the offensive and to concentrate our available resources in an attempt to reach Constantinople.

Bulgaria, on September 22nd, had given orders for a general mobilization, and we were then committed to an expedition in Salonika. We were also fighting in East Africa and in Egypt. The first Italian offensive had failed.

The Russians had been driven from the Vistula, but the Germans still had a third of their fighting forces in this area of operations, so that, if the general converging attack was carried out on the Western Front, there was every prospect of having numerical superiority at the decisive point.

1915 CAMPAIGN IN FRANCE

1. OBJECT. Our object was to co-operate with the French Tenth Army by attacking the troops of the German Sixth Army holding a line of trenches in our front from the west of Lens to La Bassée. The French, in addition to the continued offensive on a twenty-mile front from Artois south of our First Army with their Tenth Army, were to make their main attack in a northerly direction from Champagne against the German Third Army, in order to cut off the German Seventh, First and Second Armies. If this combined operation was successful, Joffre hoped to compel the Germans to retreat beyond the Meuse.

2. FACTORS affecting its attainment.

(a) Strength and Location of Opposing Forces. On our six miles of front, from the west of Lens to La Bassée, the Germans had their forward defences held by four regiments of the 14th and 117th Divisions and a Jäger battalion. Their Corps reserves were the Guards Reserve Division at Allennes and the 8th Division at Douai. Their Army reserves consisted of three divisions at Lille and Valenciennes.

We had six divisions in our forward positions, with three divisions and the Cavalry Corps and Indian Cavalry Corps in reserve. From south to north, our divisions were in the following order: 47th, 15th and 1st, of the IV Corps; then the 7th, 9th and 2nd, of the I Corps. The 21st Division was west of the IV Corps in the vicinity of Noeux-les-Mines, and the 24th Division was west of the I Corps at Beuvry and Bethune.

The Guards Division was farther west at Auchel Bois des Dames, and the 3rd Cavalry Division was in the woods four miles south-west of Bethune. The French Tenth Army, whose line ran from our right to the south of Arras for twelve miles, had six Corps, with two cavalry divisions in reserve, ready to pass through the gap in the German defences.

For their attack on the eighteen-mile front in Champagne, the French had eight Corps and six cavalry divisions.

On our front we not only had a great numerical superiority, namely, 75,000 to the Germans' 11,000, but we had four times as many field guns and howitzers and more than double the number of heavy guns than the Germans had on our actual front of attack, and also 5,028 cylinders filled with chlorine gas, and 7,870 smoke candles.

As to location, the enemy had considerably strengthened their positions since the Battle of Aubers Ridge. Behind the southern part of their line was Lens, with its suburbs, which were very strong defensive centres. Our trenches, which were about 400 yards from the Germans on the western side of the Grenay spur, could be overlooked for the most part from their Loos Road redoubts.

They had excellent means of lateral intercommunication in the Lens-La Bassée Road two miles behind their front line at Lens and one mile behind it at Cité St. Elie.

They had observation posts from which they could by day observe our movements up to our forward positions in the slag-heaps and shafts at the pitheads. Particularly valuable for this observation were the Loos Pylons and Fosse 8 close to their front lines.

Our nearest upstanding observation post was two miles from our front line. So strong were the German defences between La Bassée and Lens, that the First Army Commander strongly advised that our offensive should be carried out farther north. In addition to their very strong front line, in which were redoubts of exceptional strength, they had a second line covered with thick wire entanglements, which our field guns could not reach for wire-cutting until we had taken their first line.

An intermediate line ran north from Cité St. Edouard and west of Loos, where there was a power station which furnished the dug-outs with electric light. Elaborate telephonic systems enabled the Germans to support rapidly any point with artillery fire.

Observation posts, constructed of reinforced concrete, covered with steel cupolas, machine-gun emplacements encased in concrete, and dug-outs, 30 feet deep, were everywhere connected up with the main trenches round Loos.

Their second line ran on both sides of the Lens-La Bassée Road through the western part of Lens, west of Cité St. Auguste, Hulluch, Cité St. Elie, Haisnes, and La Bassée. Hill 70, north of Lens, was valuable for observation, and had on it a strong redoubt. North of this hill were Chalet Wood, Chalk Pit Wood, and Bois Hugo, which gave concealment to defenders, who could enfilade troops advancing east over the flat, open plain towards Hulluch and Cité St. Elie. All the cottages near the pitheads had cellars, which were converted by the Germans into strong machine-gun nests.

Owing to the difficulties of offensive operations in the area north of the Tenth Army, it was thought our operations in the plain north of Lens, and those of the French Tenth Army advancing towards Vimy, would make the German position in the easily defensible positions in and round Loos and Lens untenable, and that close support on the flank of the Tenth Army was essential to prevent the Germans concentrating their reserves and artillery against the French.

An unsupported attack by the French Tenth Army might

lead to the Germans enfilading both the flanks of this Army with heavy artillery fire, and the wider the front of attack the more dispersed the enemy must be to meet it, and the better opportunity there might be of breaking through at one point which would lead to the success of the whole operation, and, as General Foch considered, would render our two armies masters of the Plain of Douai.

(b) *Topography.* The French Tenth Army had captured the important plateau of Notre Dame de Lorette and the villages of Ablain St. Nazaire and Carency (two miles southwest of Souchez); also the works connecting Carency with La Targette (two and three-quarter miles south-east of Carency), and the Labyrinth Fortress (one a half miles south of La Targette), which is astride the Arras-Lens Road.

North of Souchez, the Germans still retained the eastern slopes of the plateau of Notre Dame de Lorette and the Bois-en-Hache, and then their positions extended north of Angres and Liévin in front of the low Loos-Hulluch-Haisnes Hills to the Bethune-La Bassée-Lille Canal near La Bassée.

The Hill of Vimy, 460 feet above sea-level, was between the French and the plain running from the Scarpe below Arras to the La Bassée-Lille Canal. The mining city is in the low ground east of Liévin and south-east of Loos. Therefore, as the French Commander pointed out, the capture of either the Loos-Hulluch-Haisnes Ridges or of the Vimy Height would cause the Germans to evacuate Lens.

The Germans, however, were strongly entrenched in Vimy, Petit Vimy, Farbus, and Thelus. East of Souchez, the slopes of Vimy Hill reach a height of 390 feet; that is, 150 feet lower than the top of Notre Dame de Lorette, from which point, however, it was not possible to gain observation over the Vimy slopes.

North-east of Neuville St. Vaast, which is just east of La Targette, the Vimy slopes are covered with the thick La Folie Woods, which gave excellent cover and concealment. The eastern slopes of Vimy Ridge fall steeply to the plain, so that on this side troops and guns close below the crest were safe from our fire.

The Germans had strengthened their positions in this area with barbed-wire entanglements, which were immune also from our artillery fire. Souchez lies in a hollow watered by the River Souchez. East of this village, the ground rises up to Hill 119, and to the village and wood of Givenchy. Hill 119 was connected up by wide, deep trenches, with Hill 140 in the La Folie Wood.

The Germans dammed up the Carency and St. Nazaire streams, making an impassable swamp west of Souchez. The approach to Souchez from the north was difficult, with the Germans holding the eastern slopes of the Notre Dame de Lorette Plateau and also the Bois-en-Hache. The approach to these places from the west could be enfiladed by German artillery in Angres and Liévin.

For the First Army, the capture of the Loos-Hulluch-Haisnes Ridge was most important. This ridge was covered with trenches supplemented by redoubts and observation posts. West of Loos were two large slag-heaps known as the Double Crassier. On the track from Vermelles to Loos was a redoubt 500 yards in diameter. Loos, a mining village, had in it a valuable observation post, known as Tower Bridge, 300 feet high. South-east of Loos on the road to Lens was a pit-shaft, also valuable for observation.

Farther east again, the ground sloped up to the Lens-La Bassée Road and up to Hill 70, on which was a strong redoubt, north of which was the 14 Bis coal mine, of which the pithead was strongly fortified, as was also the chalk pit north of it.

East of Hill 70 the ground sloped down and then up again to the village of Cité St. Auguste. Less than two miles north of Loos were the houses of Hulluch.

A mile north-east of Hulluch were stone quarries which the Germans had converted into a fortress. Half a mile east of the quarries was Cité St. Elie, a mining village on the Lens-La Bassée Road. A similar distance north-west was the Hohenzollern Redoubt, from which a strong, deep trench, called Little Willie, ran in a northerly direction for 500 yards up to Madagascar Trench, 300 yards from our front line.

South-east from the Redoubt ran Big Willie Trench for 600 yards into Quarry Trench, half-way between the quarries and our front line, and 500 yards from both of them.

The western edge of Hohenzollern Redoubt was only 200 yards from our front line. From it three communication trenches ran in an easterly direction to the 1,200 yards of trench which joined the Quarry and Madagascar Trenches. This rear line consisted of Dump Trench and Fosse Trench. Fosse 8 was a coal mine with a high and strongly defended slag-heap, 1,000 yards south of Auchy. From these slag-heaps the Germans could observe by day up to a distance of two miles behind our front lines.

Fosse 8 was joined up to Fosse Trench by a trench called Corons Alley, running round the Corons and to Dump Trench by another communication trench called Slag Alley, running along the southern side of the Dump. Auchy village was joined up to Madagascar Trench and also to Railway Redoubt by Auchy Alley, which branches into two trenches, 400 yards

1915 CAMPAIGN IN FRANCE

west of the village, which is joined up with the reserve line west of Haisnes. Their reserve trenches just west of Cité St. Elie were joined up to their forward line at Quarry Trench by St. Elie Avenue and Alley No. 1 running north of the quarries, and to the Dump and Fosse 8 by Fosse Alley, running 1,300 yards in a north-easterly direction. Eight hundred yards south of the La Bassée Canal, the Bethune-Cambrai-La Bassée Road crossed our front-line trench. Roads ran from it across the La Bassée-Lens Road through Haisnes and Douvrin.

The Vermelles-Hulluch-Pont à Vendin Road crossed our trenches, and also the main La Bassée-Lens Road, 4,800 yards south of the Canal.

Our trenches were crossed diagonally by the Bethune-Lens Road at a point 1,400 yards west of the northern point of Loos. The Lens-Carvin Road, running north-east from Lens, was the boundary between our southernmost assaulting division and the French troops.

The Bethune-Grenay-Lens railway crossed the French front line 300 yards south of its junction with our line. Behind our trenches was the La Bassée-Vermelles-Grenay Road, and farther back was part of the Bethune-Noeux-les-Mines-Aix Noulette-Arras Causeway.

Half a mile west of Grenay, the Bethune-Lens line connected with La Bassée. Our first-line trenches ran parallel with the German at distances varying from 100 to 150 yards. Between the Vermelles-Hulluch and the Bethune-Lens Roads, the ground rose slightly towards the German trenches. South of the Bethune-Lens Road, the ground sloped down towards their lines. The soil was chalky and covered with long grass where the country was open in the plain between Loos and Haisnes.

In this plain there was no cover from the enemy's observers. It was for this reason that the Commander of the First Army considered that our offensive operations would have a better chance of success if they were carried out north of the La Bassée Canal.

(*c*) *Weather* was particularly important for this battle, as we depended on the use of chlorine gas to facilitate our initial assault and to neutralize the enemy's advantage of strong positions covered by wire and supported by artillery supplied with large reserves of ammunition.

On September 24th, a westerly breeze sprang up. If this wind held, and did not exceed six to eight miles an hour, conditions would be favourable for the use of gas and smoke. At midnight, the weather forecast was favourable; accordingly all arrangements were made for the assaulting troops to form

c 2

up in the forward trenches, which were manned by 0230 hours, when all was ready for our main offensive by our six divisions.

Unfortunately, at 0500 hours, fifty minutes before the time for turning on the gas-cylinder taps, the wind had nearly died away and was north-easterly. Luckily the conditions changed again by 0540 hours, and the light breeze was now south-westerly. It was, however, a variable breeze, as at the northern end of our line it was not sufficiently strong to carry the gas cloud to the enemy's line.

West of Loos and of the Hohenzollern Redoubt, the gas did help the troops. Close to the Canal, however, the gas had to be discontinued, as the breeze was not strong enough to carry it forward. The effects of the use of gas were thus empirical and dependent entirely on the direction and strength of the wind and on the distance between our opposing lines. In the places where it reached the Germans, it caused panic; in other parts, it drifted back to our lines.

(*d*) *Time and Space.* The important distances to our objectives and from our railheads will only be considered. Our front line was approximately six miles long. The distance to our first objective between Loos and Haisnes was approximately 2,000 yards on a four-mile front.

In addition, on our northern flank the I Corps was to attack north of the La Bassée Canal towards Canteleux, halfway between La Bassée and Givenchy, and 2,000 yards from both these places. The interboundary between the IV Corps on the southern part of our front and the I Corps on the northern part was the Vermelles-Hulluch Road inclusive to the I Corps. This road crossed our front line two and three-quarter miles south of the La Bassée Canal.

The Indian Corps from the north of and excluding Givenchy were to advance towards Pietre (one mile north-east of Neuve Chapelle), and were to exploit success up to La Cliqueterie Farm (one mile south-east of Pietre). The III Corps were to break through the enemy's trenches on their front and endeavour to join up with the Indian Corps near Aubers.

Our Army reserve, consisting of the XI Corps, had two divisions about five miles behind our front line on the morning of our attack, the 3rd Cavalry Division was a further five miles back, and the 3rd Division, of the XI Corps, at Auchel aux Bois, another four miles west of the 3rd Cavalry Division. The railhead for our I Corps was at Bethune, five and a half miles west of our front line; for our IV Corps it was three miles farther west.

The XI Corps had their railhead at Lillers, seven miles north by west of Bethune. Our second objectives were on the Haute Deule Canal between and including both Courrières (six miles east-north-east of Lens) and Bauvin (four miles east of La Bassée).

Our final objective was to be the line Henin Liétard-Carvin (eight miles apart, and twelve miles from Loos to a central position between these two places).

The French Tenth Army was to attack between Ficheux (five miles south-south-west of Arras) and Lens (exclusive).

Our Cavalry Corps was to cross the Haute Deule Canal between and including both Courrières and Douai (fifteen miles north-east of Arras), and then they were to proceed to Tournai (twenty miles north-east of Douai) and to Condé (eighteen miles south-east of Tournai), and then to cut the Valenciennes (five miles south of Condé)—Ath (twenty-two miles north-east of Douai) railway and the Valenciennes-Lille (twenty miles north of Douai) railway. The cavalry advance of fifty miles would cut the enemy's communications running in a southerly direction across the Plain of Douai.

Our Second Army was to make a subsidiary attack north and south of Hooge (two and a half miles east of Ypres, and seventeen miles north of the nearest British subsidiary attack made by the III Corps).

The French Fifth Army from between Reims (ninety miles south-east of Arras) and Soissons (thirty-five miles west by north of Reims) and the French Fourth, Second and Third Armies from the west of Verdun up to the east of Reims were all to make simultaneous attacks towards Sedan (forty miles north by west of Verdun) and Mezières (fifteen miles west by north of Sedan).

3. COURSES open to the Germans were to maintain their positions on their Western Front while they concentrated on their present objective. This objective was to gain a decision against the Russians. Consequently, they strengthened their defences on their Western Front by adding a second line of trenches and joining it up to the front line, by making redoubts in their forward positions, and by making their villages very strong defensive localities.

Courses open to the B.E.F. were:

(a) To remain on the defensive until we had more than nine divisions available on the Western Front for offensive operations.

In view of our commitments in Mesopotamia, Africa, Salonika, the Dardanelles, and India, and of the necessity for keeping some troops for home defence, it would have been our more prudent course. We could then have concentrated our efforts against the Turks in the Dardanelles or at Kut. Our many subsidiary operations were a great drain on our resources in men and material, and both these would be required in the greatest possible extent to deal with the very strong line of defences as well as the fortresses and defended villages which would have to be attacked frontally by our six divisions and three divisions in reserve, of which two were New Army divisions, and had only recently arrived in the country.

(*b*) To carry out offensive operations in co-operation with the French. In view of the fact that the Allies had a numerical superiority over the Germans on their Western Front of 385,000 rifles, and that the Germans were making such progress against the Russians that they might shortly be returning to the Western front with increased *morale*, numbers of rifles and stores of ammunition, it was thought that this would be an opportunity for breaking through their front defences which might not occur again.

Once their forward lines were broken by convergent attacks from Champagne and Artois, we should be able to cut off the troops in the salient they had made in our front. The cavalry would exploit success up to the general line Mons-Namur, and then a general offensive by all the Allies would free French soil of the German invaders and, as General Joffre said, possibly end the war.

On the other hand, though we had numerical superiority, our output of gun ammunition was very much less than that of the Germans and Austrians. This would naturally give them a great advantage, especially as we could not attack on the whole front; nor could we hope to add to our output for many months, as our Ministry of Munitions had only been formed in June, 1915, and there was much organization and building of factories to be done.

We could only concentrate at points the capture of which would lead to decisive results, and then our frontal attacks would be met not only in front, but on the flanks, by heavy artillery fire, to which we could not reply on equal terms.

We hoped somewhat to neutralize this advantage by the use of gas, but this was an experiment, and depended entirely on the weather conditions.

The Germans had the advantage of observation posts from which any movements in our communication trenches could be seen by day.

The training for staff duties and leadership was not now, owing to our heavy losses, equal to the very great difficulties of command, administration and liaison required in carrying out offensive actions against an enemy behind fortifications which were very formidable at the Battle of Festubert on May 16th, 1915, and since then had been considerably strengthened.

However, we had to look beyond our own difficulties, and we had to give all the help we could to the French in the attempt to carry out a plan which had great possibilities. At Aubers and at Festubert, we had not had converging operations to distract the enemy. We had only advanced in one direction. Now, by diminishing the numbers on certain parts of our front, and by attacking in an easterly direction from Artois, and in a northerly direction from Champagne at the same time, we might in our initial operations, owing to concentrating troops in two areas, where the attack was to be pressed home at these decisive points, have a superiority in numbers of six to one in our favour, and cut off the three German Armies holding the Noyon Salient.

Our exploitation of this initial success might enable us to stop the enemy from re-forming their other Armies in rearward positions, and might give the whole Allied forces an opportunity of defeating in detail the German Armies.

PLAN. Our plan, therefore, was to carry out a continued offensive operation with the French Tenth Army between Arras and La Bassée towards Douai-Carvin.

The First Army was to take the offensive on September 25th at 0630 hours between Lens and La Bassée and break through the enemy's front lines and then advance to the Haute Deule Canal between and including Courrières and Bauvin, and then this was to be exploited up to the line Henin Liétard-Carvin. Subsidiary attacks were to be made by the Indian Corps towards Aubers and Pietre, and by the Second Army towards Hooge.

Behind the First Army, a general reserve was to be formed, consisting of the Cavalry, Indian Cavalry Corps, and XI Corps. Behind the Second Army, there was to be one division in reserve. The cavalry were to exploit success up to Condé and Tournai, and to cut the Valenciennes-Lille and Ath-Lille railways. The Royal Flying Corps were also to bomb these lines, as well as the Lille-Don, Lille-Douai, Courtrai-Deynze lines. The Dover Patrol was to co-operate by shelling the German coast batteries between Knocke and Blankenberghe and at Westende and Middleskercke, in order to mystify and mislead the enemy and make them think that a landing was intended near the Dutch frontier.

Before the infantry assault and after a four days' continuous artillery bombardment, starting on September 21st, gas was to be discharged for forty minutes if weather conditions were suitable. Phosphorous candles were to be lighted to form a thick smoke screen. The artillery was to carry out an intensive bombardment during the discharge of gas against the enemy's trenches and communications.

The details of our plan were as follow: —

The front held by the First Army was divided between the IV Corps on the south up to and exclusive of the Vermelles-Hulluch Road, and by the I Corps from and including this road up to the La Bassée Canal. The IV Corps were to attack from and including the Double Crassier on their allotted front. The I Corps were to attack on the remainder of the front up to the La Bassée Canal. North of the Canal also an attack was to be carried out by a brigade in the vicinity of Givenchy towards Canteleux.

Our main attack was to be carried out by the four central divisions, namely, the 15th, 1st, 7th and 9th, and two brigades of the 2nd Division, in order to break through the enemy's positions between Double Crassier and the Canal, and then to capture Loos, Hill 70, Cité St. Auguste, and the whole of the enemy's second line up to Hulluch, Cité St. Elie, Haisnes, and Canal Alley Trench running along the railway from the Canal to the north of Haisnes.

The southern flank was to be protected by the 47th Division operating against the enemy between Double Crassier and Loos.

Our further objectives were to be Pont à Vendin and the Lens-Carvin Road for the IV Corps, while the I Corps were to secure the Haute Deule Canal up to and including Bauvin. In the IV Corps, the 15th and 1st Divisions were to carry out the main attack. The 15th Division, after breaking through the enemy's front line, was to attack Loos, then Hill 70 and then Cité St. Auguste.

Farther north, the 1st Division, after reaching the Lens-La Bassée Road, was to take Bois Hugo and the southern part of Hulluch. North of the 1st Division, the 7th Division was to advance on a 1,400-yard front through the enemy's front trenches, and to take the Quarries, Cité St. Elie, and the northern part of Hulluch.

The 9th Division was to attack on a 1,500-yard front, and had to capture Hohenzollern Redoubt, the Dump, and Fosse 8 before attacking the German second line and Haisnes, and then press on with the 7th Division to the Haute Deule Canal. The 2nd Division had to operate with its three brigades on a frontage of 3,500 yards.

After the capture of Auchy, a defensive flank was to be formed along the Canal Alley Trench south of the Canal. North of the Canal, the 5th Brigade was to continue its defensive flank back to our original line through Canteleux, to join up with the Indian Corps farther north.

The result of these plans on the first day of our attack was that everywhere on our front except in the northern sector on either side of the La Bassée Canal we had been able to break through the enemy's front line of trenches. West of Hulluch, and north and south of the Hulluch-Vermelles Road, our troops had reached the Lens-La Bassée Road. West of Haisnes, the 26th and 27th Brigades had gained a footing in the enemy's second-line trenches. Our troops had captured prisoners and guns, and had dealt severely with the enemy.

The French Army, who attacked six and a half hours after our zero hour, was able to make progress on their left flank south of our line. Unfortunately, our casualties during the day had been heavy, and there were many gaps in the positions which we had gained. Our reserves had not been near enough to the front line to exploit the successes when we gained them, and the Germans had been able to bring twenty-two fresh battalions into the battle area to strengthen their positions by September 26th.

The results obtained did not, as hoped, counter-balance the successes which the Germans and Austrians had won over the Russians, and for which they had weakened their Western Front, in order to gain a numerical superiority at the place where they wanted to obtain a decision. It had been for this reason that the French had wished to take the offensive while there was a numerical superiority on the Western Front.

Between success and disappointing results, there must always be a small dividing line. Had the head of the XI Corps been in a position to exploit the success and to carry on the momentum of the attacking divisions when an advance of two miles at one point had been made on the morning of September 25th, we might have broken through the German second line on a broad front. Success then might have meant local victory, as the German reserves were not at hand.

A local victory might have enabled us to cut off the Germans who were fighting in front of the French Tenth Army. During the morning and afternoon, the Germans were actually making preparations to evacuate the country for many miles east of the line we had broken through between Loos and Auchy.

The Germans had to bring two regiments of their 8th Division by rail and motor to a position three and a half miles east of Lens. Then one of these regiments had to march to Cité St. Laurent and to positions between the redoubt on Hill 70 and to Loos Crassier, while the other regiment took up positions near Bois Hugo and Chalet Wood.

To safeguard their northern flank, two Guard Reserve Regiments were sent up during the afternoon of the 25th by train to places respectively three miles east of Hulluch and seven miles east of La Bassée, and then they had to march to the Haisnes-St. Elie sector of their defences. Later in the evening, three battalions were sent up by rail from Armentières to Haisnes, and one battalion marched to a position three and a quarter miles east by south of La Bassée.

By 1800 hours on September 25th, all the battalions of our reserves, namely, the XI Corps, had not reached their allotted positions of deployment east of the Vermelles-Grenay Road. Their orders for a further advance did not reach their brigade headquarters till after 0200 hours on September 26th.

By this time, the German second line was held more strongly than their first line had been during our initial assaults.

Before the close of this battle, on October 8th, we had advanced our line on a front of 8,000 yards at its farthest point to approximately 3,200 yards; we had captured approximately 3,000 prisoners, 26 guns, and 40 machine guns, and we had taken " localities fortified at leisure by all the experience and skill of the German engineers."[*]

In the Special Order of the Day, the Commander-in-Chief, with reference to this battle, wrote: " I desire to express to the Army under my command my deep appreciation of the splendid work they have accomplished. Old Army, New Army and Territorials have vied with one another in the heroic conduct displayed throughout the battle by officers, N.C.Os. and men. I feel the utmost confidence and assurance that the same glorious spirit which has been so marked a feature throughout the first phase of this great battle will continue until our efforts are crowned by final and complete victory."

---

[*] Official History of the War, Vol. IV.

CHAPTER II.

BATTLE OF AUBERS RIDGE, MAY 9TH, 1915, ILLUSTRATING F.S.R.

IN this battle, there were two attacks. There was a southern attack, in which the I and Indian Corps made two assaults in an easterly direction, and a northern attack, in which the IV Corps made an assault in a south-easterly direction. The total front to be attacked by the brigades of the I, Indian and IV Corps detailed for the first operation following the bombardment was 3,900 yards. This was in accordance with our Regulations: —

"In the case of a frontal attack it will seldom be possible to attack on the whole front; the covering fire available for the support of the attack must be concentrated and the attack of the infantry driven home on those portions of the front on which fire is so concentrated; the extent of these will depend on the amount of resistance anticipated, and the resources available."

To support the I Corps, we had 142 guns and howitzers. To support the Indian Corps, we had three field brigades and 36 howitzers.

In our Regulations it is stated that: —

"Surprise is the first and most important principle to be considered in planning an attack, and hence for the opening phase a preliminary bombardment of more than a few minutes will rarely be advisable."

In this battle, at 0500 hours the bombardment began; it became intensive half an hour later, and then, at 0540 hours, the leading battalions of the 2nd and 3rd Brigades of the 1st Division left the front-line trenches. The Germans were not surprised. They had been expecting an attack after the thirty minutes' artillery fire, and were manning their front-line parapets.

Our men were received with heavy rifle and machine-gun fire as they began to leave the trenches. Therefore, our casualties were very heavy before we were able to establish a position eighty yards from the enemy's front trenches. On the front of the Dehra Dun Brigade north of the 3rd Brigade, so heavy was the enemy's rifle and machine-gun fire that the troops, as they left their trenches, suffered too severely to make any further advance possible.

In F.S.R. it is stated that:—
"Counter-battery work will form an important part of the artillery plan. The object to aim at is to neutralize all hostile batteries which by their fire can impede the advance of the infantry."

Ten minutes after the first assault from our trenches, there was another attempt on the part of the 2nd, 3rd and Dehra Dun Brigades to reach the enemy's positions, but again we were unsuccessful, as the artillery had not in the time and with the ammunition available been able to neutralize the German fire power. Nor was machine-gun fire superimposed on any part of the artillery barrage to increase its intensity and depth, as advocated in F.S.R. 74 (4).

The result was that our advancing lines suffered heavily from frontal and enfilade machine-gun fire, and the few men who managed to get through the gaps made in the wire were unable to get a footing in the enemy's front-line trenches.

The organizing of further assaults now became difficult, owing to the fact that there were a number of our wounded close to the enemy's wire, and owing to the forward trenches being congested with casualties, so that our artillery was not able to cut the enemy's wire or to silence their machine guns. Our attacks, after the further ten minutes' bombardment, were made at some points against the same objectives which in the first attack had failed.

This is not in accordance with Field Service Regulations, in which it is advocated that local reserves should be directed against "such points as appear to offer the greatest chance of success." Where we had failed in the first instance, the enemy were seen to be very strong, and there was no chance of surprising them in a second attack after another bombardment, which would warn them of an impending attack. The result was that this second assault failed completely.

In F.S.R. 29 it is stated that "detailed and timely information is a necessary factor of success in war." The Commander of the First Army was unaware of the actual position after our first assaults had failed.

Accordingly, he ordered that the attacks should be repeated at midday. Our losses had been very heavy, our front and communication trenches were being constantly bombarded, so that the movement necessary to relieve the weakened brigades in the front line was slow and costly.

The counter-battery work, which forms an important part of the artillery plan to neutralize all hostile batteries which by their fire can impede the advance of the infantry [F.S.R. 66], could not be effective, owing to the difficulties of observation. The result was that our casualties increased considerably, and there was so much confusion in the trenches leading up to the starting line, owing to the enemy's artillery fire, that zero had to be postponed for four hours. Fresh battalions were then to carry out the assault, namely, two battalions both from the 1st and 3rd Brigades, and two battalions from the Bareilly Brigade of the Indian Corps.

F.S.R. 60 states that:—

"The first important factor making for success in the attack is a sound and simple general plan, the second is good co-operation between the various components of the force ordered to put the plan into effect. The time required to make the necessary preparations for the attack will differ with each of the arms of the service employed, and this must be taken into consideration before the time for the launching of the attack can be decided."

Fifteen minutes before zero hour, the commanding officer of one of the battalions of the 1st Brigade detailed for the assault reported that, owing to delays in advancing up trenches down which the 2nd Brigade was withdrawing, it would not be able to form up at the time appointed for the attack. Thus on the front of the 1st Brigade there was a lack of co-operation.

One battalion carried out the original order and attacked at zero hour. The other battalion carried out the order to attack as soon as possible. The result was that their first attack with one and a half companies was started a few minutes after zero hour, and the remainder of this battalion did not reach its starting line till forty minutes after zero hour, when the rest of the attacking troops had definitely failed to reach their first objective.

The following paragraph from F.S.R. is applicable to the final attack launched in this battle:—

"Infantry is still the only arm which can complete a victory and consolidate and hold the ground won. But whereas the vulnerability of advancing infantry remains unchanged, the destructive power of modern weapons tends ever to increase. A well-armed and resolute enemy cannot be overcome unless superiority of fire is ensured; the mere weight of the infantry assault will not of itself be effective."

Our first attacking battalion of the 1st Brigade advanced with the greatest possible determination, and a few men were able to get past the German front line to their support trenches before the enemy's machine guns were able to stop completely the advance of the supporting companies and to annihilate those who had been able to advance beyond their front trenches.

Of the one and a half companies that attacked, the German machine gunners accounted for over half their numbers before they were half-way to their objective, and for two-thirds of their numbers before they were checked a little farther on in " No Man's Land " when this second frontal attack failed, owing to the destructive power of the enemy's modern weapons.

Similarly, on the front of the 3rd Brigade, the two attacking battalions suffered very heavily from the enemy's machine guns as soon as they left their forward trenches. Our leading troops were not able to advance more than 100 yards from their starting place.

On the front of the Indian Corps, our casualties began to be considerable even before our advance started from the front trenches. Throughout our bombardment, the enemy had been able to keep up heavy machine-gun fire, so that, when we started to advance in the open, and our bombardment ceased, the enemy's fire became so intense that the bulk of our troops who tried to advance were killed or wounded close to their starting point. Forty minutes after zero hour all further efforts of the I and Indian Corps were stopped.

We had not sufficient guns and ammunition to deal with the enemy's machine guns and batteries to enable us to gain " the necessary superiority of fire over a well-armed resolute enemy." Similar conditions occurred on the front of the IV Corps. Our frontal attacks were dealt with by the unshaken fire of the German 16th and 21st Reserve Regiments.

Though we had a superiority in numbers of possibly some 5,000 men, we could not counterbalance the advantage which the enemy had in strength of position and in numbers of machine guns. To support the 7th Division in its attack, 109 guns and howitzers were available to cut wire and to deal with communication trenches, but the advance of our infantry was met with such heavy fire that forty minutes after zero the attacking troops were definitely checked in " No Man's Land." The plan had been ambitious and not quite in accordance with the relative armament, training and *morale* of the opposing forces, as laid down in F.S.R. 6.

The 8th Division was to advance in an easterly direction on a front of 1,400 yards towards Fromelles, one and a quarter miles from the starting point; then, when they had passed through their first objective, the 7th Division was to continue in a south-easterly direction towards Aubers, nearly one and a half miles east of the German front-line trenches. Our troops, however, were only able to gain a footing in the enemy's forward trenches at three points, where they were cut off and isolated.

The remainder of the attacking troops were unable, owing to the enemy's machine-gun fire, to make any movement in "No Man's Land."

"Success in the infantry attack depends in the first instance on fire which makes movement possible." [F.S.R. 65 (1).]

Our artillery was not able to silence the enemy's machine guns, much of our ammunition was defective, and the guns also had suffered by excessive use, and so our troops as they started their attack came under very heavy fire, which was continued as they tried to cross the few hundred yards of open ground in front of the German trenches. That a few of our men did actually enter the German front line was marvellous, but it could lead to no definite result, as they could not be supported.

The further attacks of the 24th and 25th Brigades ordered by the First Army Commander could not materialize, owing to heavy casualties in our communication trenches making forward movement to the starting point difficult, and owing to the accurate fire of the enemy against any troops who were in the open.

In F.S.R. it is stated that "a time will probably come in every attack when the advance can only be continued by the intervention of fresh troops." Such a time had now come. At 2000 hours, the First Army Commander decided to break off the battle.

CHAPTER III

Battle of Festubert, May 15th to 25th, 1915, illustrating F.S.R.

The results in this battle were more encouraging than those obtained on May 9th. Our method of attack was somewhat changed, as we substituted longer and more systematic bombardments for short and intensive ones, which had been unsatisfactory in the Battle of Aubers Ridge. However, we suffered in comparison wih the Germans from a shortage in heavy artillery, mortars and grenades. In spite of this lack of equipment for trench warfare, we did gain considerable success, as the enemy were forced to withdraw in many places from their forward positions, which they had spent much time and labour to strengthen.

Much had been learnt from the Battle of Aubers Ridge.

The plan for the Battle of Festubert was not so ambitious; there was more co-ordination between the attacking divisions, and the objectives were not so distant.

The orders for the battle were received in good time for all to understand thoroughly the general plan and the objectives and to work out the details as to frontages, tasks, reinforcements, and evacuations.

F.S.R. 72 (8) states that "Orders for a deliberate attack should reach infantry brigade headquarters not less than 48 hours before zero hour."

For this battle, the operation orders were issued to units on May 13th for the attack, which was started by 10,000 men of the 5th, 6th and Garhwal Brigades at 2330 hours on May 15th.

The Commander of the 2nd Division decided to effect surprise and to avoid observation and hostile fire, by night operations.

F.S.R. states that:—

"Success in all night operations depends on a thorough reconnaissance by day and, when possible, by night, on simplicity of plan, security from hostile air observation and attack, and on minute preliminary preparations by commanders and staffs concerned."

The attackers of the 6th Brigade, by carrying out these principles, were able to gain the advantage of surprise. This brigade attacked on the southern front of the 2nd Division, north of it was the 5th Brigade, and then came the Garhwal Brigade. These three brigades on a frontage of 1,700 yards were, in the first instance, to advance approximately 1,000 yards to La Quinque Rue.

In spite of the fact that the German front-line trench was only 300 yards away, and that a dyke, 12 feet wide, had to be crossed, so excellent were the preliminary arrangements that the 6th Brigade reached the German front-line trenches without a shot being fired; and then the supporting companies passed through and consolidated the captured ground behind the forward German trenches.

Thus they carried out the principle contained in F.S.R.:—

"Each successive objective should be attacked by freshly organized and complete units, which should be made responsible for the consolidation of the objective when gained. The capture of any important tactical feature or locality must be made the task of a definite unit."

The brigades north of the 6th Brigade lost the advantage of surprise, as the bursts of rifle and machine-gun fire at intervals preceding zero hour from the Jullundur Brigade farther north had made the Germans alert. When the 5th and Garhwal Brigades began to advance, the Germans illuminated "No Man's Land," and brought heavy artillery, machine-gun and rifle fire to bear on all the troops in it.

The result was that only one half-battalion was able to reach the German front trench close to the left of the 6th Brigade, whose flanks were now exposed.

"Success must be followed up until the enemy's power is crushed." [F.S.R. 76 (1).]

After the failure to reach the whole front on La Quinque Rue, orders were issued to renew the frontal attack four and a quarter hours after the original zero hour against the front of the enemy's position where we had been unsuccessful. During this time, the enemy had ample opportunity to reorganize and prepare for our further attacks. There was no surprise possible.

The Garhwal Brigade, starting at 0315 hours, lost so heavily as they left their parapets that no advance could be made. The 5th Brigade had not had time to form up after their heavy losses in the original attack, and so could not start at the time arranged for a simultaneous assault at 0315 hours with the 7th Division.

The following paragraph from F.S.R. was carefully carried out in the opening phase of this battle:—

"The plan of attack will include the allotment of the artillery resources to the various tasks of bombardment, harassing fire, counter-battery work, barrage fire, and close support at various stages of the artillery preparation and of the attack. Counter-battery work will form an important part of the artillery plan. The object to aim at is to neutralize all hostile batteries which by their fire can impede the advance of the infantry."

Our thirty-six hours' bombardment, which was later continued for a further twenty-four hours, started early on May 13th. Slow and carefully observed fire was brought to bear on the German forward parapets, wire, rear trenches and batteries for three periods of two hours daily on May 13th and 14th. At night, firing was continued to prevent the enemy from bringing up reinforcements and supplies, and from mending their wire.

For the very close support of the attack of the 7th Division, six guns were brought up to our front line during the night of May 14th/15th. For the attack of the 7th Division, the principles in the following paragraph, of F.S.R., were carried out:—

"In the case of a frontal attack, it will seldom be possible to attack on the whole front; the covering fire available for the support of the attack must be concentrated; the extent of these will depend on the amount of resistance anticipated, and the resources available. In selecting the portions of the front for the main attack the commander must aim at definite tactical advantages."

The plan for the 7th Division was to attack on a frontage of 850 yards with two brigades. Each brigade was given definite objectives, some 1,200 yards south-east of their starting line. In three and three-quarter hours after zero, three battalions of the 22nd Brigade reached their objectives, but, owing to heavy enfilade machine-gun and rifle fire, their casualties had been heavy. Their left flank was exposed, and they had suffered too heavily to make a further advance.

Our Regulations advocate that:—

"Every effort should be made to increase the gap caused by successful penetration at one point of the enemy's position."

Had reserves been available at this juncture to exploit the success of the 22nd Brigade, who had reached North Breastwork and the Orchard, great results might have been obtained, as the Germans had sent their local reserves away from the area in front of the 22nd Brigade, and a further advance might have been easily carried out without creating too pronounced a salient.

F.S.R. is applicable to this situation, namely:—

"Premature employment of brigade and divisional reserves must be avoided, but immediately a commander sees that substantial progress is being made, reserves must be pushed forward to confirm the success, to protect exposed flanks or to relieve units which have suffered in the advance."

In this case, at 0700 hours, when the 22nd Brigade had gained their objective, further substantial progress might have been made had reserves been available to confirm the success.

North of the 22nd Brigade, the 20th Brigade started their assault five minutes before zero hour. F.S.R. states that:—

"In order to gain full advantage from the protection of a creeping barrage, it is essential that the leading infantry should keep close behind it throughout their advance, and should assault each hostile position immediately the fire of the artillery has lifted from it."

The two leading battalions of the 20th Brigade suffered heavily by following too closely behind the barrage, as they did not wait for the bombardment to lift from the enemy's trenches. However, they managed to reach their objectives.

The Germans now carried out the following principles enunciated in F.S.R. 82 (2):—

"If portions of an attacking force succeed in penetrating the defender's position, they usually become more or less disorganized owing to casualties and to the fact that they are operating on unfamiliar ground. With well-trained troops, and in an attack which has been methodically prepared, this disorganization will only be temporary, but the period of disorganization offers to the defenders a fleeting opportunity for engaging the enemy when he is at a great disadvantage. An immediate counter-attack may succeed in restoring the situation and inflicting heavy casualties on the attacking troops."

The left flank of the northern battalion of the 20th Brigade, on reaching its first objective, was enfiladed by machine-gun fire, and then the Germans made a counter-attack in front and on the flank against our depleted ranks. The Germans were checked by a support company of the 20th Brigade, and by 0900 hours this brigade was able to maintain a position in the vicinity of the German original front line.

The dangers of an advance by assaulting troops with a

gap between their inner flanks was exemplified in this operation. Although both divisions of the I Corps were able to advance, they were not able, by 0900 hours, to close the gap between the leading troops of the divisions who reached their first objective. The Germans between them were then able to enfilade the inner flanks of the assaulting brigades of the 2nd and 7th Divisions.

The difficulty of closing this gap during daylight on May 16th was that the enemy's fire was so heavy and accurate that troops were unable to advance across the open, and the communication trench leading across " No Man's Land " was practically blocked by wounded, and, though no battalion of the 22nd Brigade was able to gain ground in a southerly direction, neither of the inner brigades of the 7th and 2nd Divisions could gain ground towards one another. The fact that our guns could not silence the enemy's batteries about Lorgies, two and a half miles east of our front line at the junction between the 20th and 22nd Brigades, made the chances of a further successful advance by the Indian Corps doubtful.

The plan for May 17th, therefore, was for the I Corps to close the gap in their front along La Quinque Rue, and then to bring their left flank back in a north-westerly direction to join up with the Indian Corps on their original line. Our Regulations bring out the necessity of synchronizing attacks and of making them simultaneous, if that is the intention, by careful previous arrangements, as obviously unconnected disjointed blows are not so effective as those that are concentrated at the decisive time and place.

However, in this case, the two assaulting battalions of the 21st Brigade south of the gap attacked half an hour before the 6th Brigade on the north of the gap, owing to the change in the time of zero hour being advanced half an hour. In spite of this, the two divisions before midday on the 17th were able to advance on La Quinque Rue, which was then to be consolidated preparatory to an advance on Violaines, approximately 2,500 yards east of the first objective.

This procedure is in accordance with F.S.R.:—

" Unless the enemy is in full retreat the position gained must be firmly consolidated against counter-attack, and the assaulting troops made ready to renew the attack."

Later again the attacks of the 2nd and 7th Divisions were not simultaneous; there was an interval of an hour between them. This led to one battalion running into the artillery fire which was preparing the way for an advance by the other division. These two attacks had to be abandoned. The Guards Brigade was then to support the further attacks, but, owing to the state of the communication trenches, it was only able to reach the line held by the 21st Brigade by 2100 hours, when the positions gained were consolidated.

Our lack of success in our attempt to capture South Breastwork at 1930 hours was due largely to topographical difficulties. In F.S.R. 32 (6) it is stated that "Time spent in reconnaissance is rarely wasted." The 400 yards of "No Man's Land" between our trenches on the right of the 21st Brigade and the enemy's line at South Breastwork was intersected with dykes. These obstacles were unknown to our troops, and, although a small party had been able to reach the South Breastwork, they had lost all their bombs during their advance through the dykes, and later were forced by hostile counter-attacks to withdraw.

On the 18th the attacks were to be continued by two new brigades—the 3rd Canadian Brigade and the 4th Guards Brigade—towards Ferme Cour d'Avoué and to a point about 1,200 yards south of it. The Germans, however, had ample time in which to strengthen their new line unknown to us, nor was there any possibility of surprising them, as the attack by the Guards was not started until 1630 hours. The enfilade fire brought to bear by the Germans caused such heavy casualties that the advance could not be carried out. The other assaulting brigade was not able to start an attack until an hour after the Guards Brigade had been checked.

Owing to the difficulties of synchronizing these attacks, and owing to the strength of the enemy's positions and the defenders' readiness, little progress could be made on the 18th.

The Canadian and 71st Divisions relieved the 7th and 2nd Divisions of the I Corps by the morning of May 20th. But during this time, the Germans were also bringing up fresh troops and were strengthening their positions. Thus, although there was excellent co-operation on May 24th by the southern brigade of the Canadian Division and the northern brigade of the 47th Division in their attack at 0230 hours, our advance was slow and costly, and where we did gain a footing we had to withdraw again before daylight, as the enemy were well supplied with grenades, and they had local reserves at hand.

The following F.S.R. paragraph was applicable to the German use of their machine-guns:—

"The value of a sudden and violent burst of machine-gun fire against the flanks of an enemy who has succeeded in penetrating the defences cannot be overestimated, and a proportion of guns should usually be located in concealed positions for this purpose."

On the following night, the deadly effect of unshaken enfilade machine-gun fire was again shown when another attack took place by the 47th and Canadian Divisions, starting at 1830 hours from the Givenchy-Chapelle St. Roch Road to the South Breastwork.

Our casualties were heavy during the advance to the German trenches, both from machine guns and from their heavy guns, which were out of reach of the guns supporting our troops and also later when we reached their trenches, owing to our shortage of grenades with which to repel the German counter-attack.

During the following days, our divisions held the positions which they had gained, in spite of the enemy's counter-attacks, in accordance with the following principle of F.S.R. 83 (1): —

"Troops which succeed in maintaining their positions in spite of hostile successes on their flanks are of the utmost assistance in dislocating an enemy's organization, in breaking up his attack, and in assisting counter-attacks."

And, in F.S.R. 77 (3): —

"For all troops actually allotted to the defence of any locality, there is, as far as they are concerned, only one degree of resistance; that is, to the last round and the last man."

Orders were issued on May 25th that the offensive operations of the First Army should be abandoned.

CHAPTER IV.

THE BATTLE OF LOOS EXAMINED IN RELATION TO THE FIELD SERVICE REGULATIONS.

THE main lessons of the Battle of Loos, fought between September 25th and October 16th, 1915, were:—

(a) The attack on a limited front against an enemy in very strong positions will lead to indecisive results, unless reserves are at hand to exploit success.

(b) The necessity of maintaining at every point the momentum of the attack until the objective is gained.

(c) The necessity of close liaison and co-operation to prevent salients being formed and open flanks being left after a temporary success.

(d) The necessity of a vast amount of heavy artillery and a large supply of shells of all kinds and of mortars and grenades if an attack is to be made in daylight across open ground against very strong, well-sited trenches.

(e) The standard of leadership must be very high in all ranks, and the discipline among the troops must be very firm, to deal with the many unforeseen incidents and checks in an advance across the open against entrenched positions.

(f) The training also of all ranks requires to be very high, in order to maintain direction in the advance and the assault, so that objectives are not mistaken and gaps are not formed in the assaulting lines, and so that initiative is shown in the use of local reserves to exploit success.

(g) The necessity for thorough staff work to enable troops to reach their starting lines with the minimum of hardship and discomfort, so that reserve divisions arrive in the best fighting condition.

(h) The necessity as to a clear understanding of the use of the reserves. In this battle, there was not a concentration of the general reserves at the decisive point, after the local reserves of the first-line attacking troops had been used up on the understanding that the general reserves would be available to exploit their initial success. An opportunity was thus lost of breaking through the German second line before their reserves arrived.

F.S.R. states: "With large forces there can be little, if any, hope of being able to strike with the general reserve at the right moment unless its place of concentration is determined with reference to the approximate place in which it is to be used, and the communications available.

"In such circumstances, therefore, it is essential to make this decision as early as possible, and to place the general reserve accordingly."

At 0900 hours on September 25th, when the divisions had used up their local reserves, the head of our general reserve divisions was six miles from the area in which it was required to be used.

(i) The difficulty of pressing through a second strongly entrenched position, in which the enemy are prepared for an attack, unless there is a large preponderance of ammunition. Otherwise, there will be heavy losses and little result. In this battle we lost 50,380 men.

(j) The value of consolidation after any check in an assault. This was done at Loos Crassier, and at Hill 70.

(k) The difficulties incurred in trying to break through, in one battle, a whole defensive position disposed in depth, when the enemy has power to manœuvre in rear and has time to bring up his reserves from areas where he is not engaged, will always lead to unnecessary losses.

NARRATIVE.

In this Battle of Loos, the enemy occupied a position on a frontage of approximately six miles, from the Canal two miles on the west of La Bassée to the west of the Double Crassier strong point and slag-heap, two miles north-west of Lens. The work on their whole position had been carried out for several months, so that its double line was very strong. Some of the tactical points had been artificially strengthened. On the northern part of their line, a thousand yards south of Auchy and a mile west of Haisnes, is a slag-heap called Fosse 8, a few hundred yards east of their first line. From this position all the country up to the Hohenzollern Redoubt could be commanded.

This redoubt was a mile and a quarter west of Cité St. Elie. Its western edge was a thousand yards west of Fosse 8, and

1915 CAMPAIGN IN FRANCE

was connected to it with communication trenches. This gave depth to their position, as advocated in our Field Service Regulations:

"In view of the protracted nature of position warfare it must be anticipated that the enemy will sooner or later concentrate powerful forces of artillery, mortars, and other mechanical means of destruction. Distribution of the defence in depth is, therefore, of added importance; firstly, because it tends to conceal the actual dispositions of the defenders, and so reduces losses, and secondly, because the weight of the attack may be such that it will shatter the more forward defences which are exposed to concentrated artillery and mortar fire. To obtain the necessary depth a defensive system in position warfare should consist of: (i) a forward or covering zone; (ii) a main zone."

The Germans had carried out these principles by having their forward line continued south from Hohenzollern Redoubt to Loos Redoubt on the top of a ridge three-quarters of a mile north-west of Loos. Then their covering line was continued south to include the large slag-heap, Double Crassier, a mile and a half east of Grenay. Their next series of positions parallel to their first line in this area, in which the Loos battle is concerned, ran from east of Auchy 1,500 yards to the north of the Dump; then from the Quarries, 1,000 yards west of Cité St. Elie, some trenches ran south for 1,500 yards.

The western side of Loos was covered by some 2,500 yards of trenches. Their main second line of trenches ran from the west of La Bassée to the west of Haisnes, then west of Cité St. Elie, Hulluch, Cité St. Auguste, and Lens. Hill 70, north of Lens and east of Loos, was strongly defended.

Communication trenches ran from their second line to join up Auchy with the Dump: this was called Fosse Alley. The communication trench running into the Quarries, to their first line from west of Hulluch, was called Alley 4.

Their rear defensive systems were organized on similar principles to those in front. They were, as advocated in F.S.R. 88 (6), sufficiently far in rear of the forward defences to cause our attacking troops to organize a distinct operation to attack them.

North of Hulluch their second line was approximately 2,000 yards east of our front line. Between Lens and Hulluch it was approximately another 2,000 yards farther east. The principles, as laid down in F.S.R. 88 (7), were also carried out.

Their continuous lines of trenches joining their posts and

localities were linked up with communication trenches in order to obtain adequate forward and lateral communications for purposes of control and maintenance. Their wiring was done in " accordance with a co-ordinated tactical plan." [F.S.R. 88.]

In the case of our attacking troops, F.S.R. may be quoted as being applicable to the forming-up positions before our attack, which started at 0630 hours on September 25th:

"Maintenance of direction is of the utmost importance. Whenever possible the line of advance should be at right angles to the forming-up positions, so that all units move straight to their front and keep the same frontage throughout."

Our IV and I Corps faced and attacked due east. The difficulty was to allot to units equal tasks. In some areas there were very formidable posts and localities which would take longer to capture and to clear than the areas where the fortifications were not so strong. For instance, the division on the right of the I Corps had no Hohenzollern Redoubt or Fosse 8 in their front, and so they were able to push on more quickly than the division on their left.

In three and a half hours, the right division had gained the Quarries and Cité St. Elie, and were up to Haisnes. This brings out the difficulty of carrying out the principles in F.S.R.: "Units must be strong enough to capture, clear, and consolidate the area allotted to them."

In this case, there was very heavy fighting by the brigade which had to capture Fosse 8, and by the brigade which had to gain the German forward trenches beyond the Vermelles-La Bassée railway, as our advancing troops were enfiladed from the enemy's defences at Auchy.

The result was that flanks on this part of the front became exposed, and salients were formed in our line, when one brigade was fighting at Fosse 8 and another east of it on the Hulluch-La Bassée Road, so that by midday our line in the north ran from Cité St. Elie to the west of the Quarries, then north to the east of the Hohenzollern Redoubt.

Farther south, the attack was carried out by the IV Corps, co-operating with the French Tenth Army, who were to start their attacks against the Germans in the vicinity of Souchez, three and a half miles south of the Franco-British boundary. This Corps attacked the Germans on a front of 6,000 yards from east of Grenay up to the Vermelles-Hulluch Road. Their right-flank division was then to form a defensive flank east of Double Crassier and the Loos Crassier, while the two

1915 CAMPAIGN IN FRANCE

northern divisions advanced to their second objectives against Hill 70, Cité St. Auguste, and Hulluch and the intervening second-line German trenches before attacking their final objectives on the Haute Deule Canal.

Their division on the south had in their front the Double Crassier and Loos. The next division of the IV Corps farther north had in its front the Loos Redoubt. The remainder of the frontage to be attacked by the IV Corps was allotted to the 1st Division.

Thus the principle, as laid down in F.S.R., namely, " The capture of any important tactical feature or locality must be made the task of a definite unit," was carried out. The basis of our plan was for the I Corps to turn the La Bassée salient from the south. The success of the IV Corps would enable the French to capture Lens, as well as the troops in Liévin and Angres, and the northern end of Vimy Heights. The French Tenth Army might then gain access to the Scheldt Plain, where mobile warfare might once more be possible.

The IV Corps, in order to reach the heights between Lens and Hulluch, had units definitely allotted for taking the Loos Redoubt, the Double Crassier, Chalk Pit, Puits 14 bis, the redoubt on the north-east corner of Hill 70, and its summit.

In the I Corps, similarly, there were detailed definite objectives. Its left wing was to push along the Canal to Auchy, to capture Haisnes, and to take in reverse Pit 8 and Hohenzollern Redoubt. The centre was to deal with Hohenzollern Redoubt and the Pit 8, while the 7th Division on the right was to capture Cité St. Elie, Quarries, and the northern part of Hulluch.

Our plan had been based on a " detailed knowledge of the relative strengths, armament, training and morale of the opposing forces " [F.S.R.], as, on the morning of September 25th, our six divisions at the disposal of the First Army Commander and the general reserves, consisting of the 21st Division at Noeux-les-Mines, the 24th Division at Beuvry and Bethune, the 3rd Cavalry Division in the Bois des Dames east of Auchel, and the Guards Division at Auchel, were immediately opposed by a Jäger battalion and four regiments of the German 14th and 117th Divisions of their Sixth Army. The nearest German reserves to the area of our main attacks were the 2nd Guards Reserve Division at Allennes, seven miles north-east of Haisnes, and their 8th Division six miles east of Souchez. It was hoped that the subsidiary attacks of our III Corps and the Lahore and Meerut Divisions might divert these reserves from the I and IV Corps fronts of attack.

F.S.R. state that "a bombardment may be necessary if there is wire or any other obstacle to be destroyed and no other means of carrying out the destruction."

In this case, the German positions were heavily covered by wire, but so carefully had our bombardments been carried out that even in front of Loos, where the German reserve lines were, their entanglements had been in places destroyed by indirect fire. This bombardment, carried out systematically all through September 24th, facilitated our advance, where the wire was cut, on the 25th. Also the following principles, as laid down in F.S.R., were carefully adhered to. The attacking infantry were deployed in close proximity to the enemy's forward defences before the moment fixed for the attack began, at distances from 400 yards on the south-east of Grenay to increasing distances to 500 yards in front of the division attacking north of the Loos Redoubt road, and decreasing to 100 yards south of the Canal.

"The success or failure of the whole operation may well depend upon the manner in which the approach march and deployment are carried out. The preparation and execution of this forward movement demand, therefore, the utmost care on the part of the staff and subordinate commanders." [F.S.R.]

In this case, no approach march on zero day was necessary, but the remainder of the paragraph was applicable to the preparation for this attack, for which all these points had been adequately arranged by 0630 hours on September 25th on the whole front of our I and IV Corps between Grenay and the La Bassée Canal.

On the northern part of our line, in the vicinity of the Canal, the careful initial staff work enabled the brigade west of the Dump to capture the German forward trenches in their first attack, in spite of the heavy enfilade fire from the higher ground at Auchy. They were also able to advance beyond the Vermelles-La Bassée railway. The brigade west of the Hohenzollern Redoubt was successful, too, owing to the accurate artillery bombardment of the interior of this redoubt, and also on Fosse 8, in spite of the enemy's accurate machine-gun fire over ground containing no cover for attacking troops.

For the employment of the remaining brigade of the 9th Division, the following paragraph is applicable:

"Premature employment of brigade and divisional reserves must be avoided, but immediately a commander sees that substantial progress is being made, reserves must be pushed forward to confirm success, to protect exposed flanks, or to relieve units which have suffered in the advance. A time will probably come in every attack when the advance can only be continued by the intervention of fresh troops." [F.S.R.]

When Fosse 8 had been captured, the troops there had their left flank open. The reserve brigade was accordingly brought up to clear the ground in the vicinity, so that by midday we had gained a line east of the redoubt and of Fosse 8 to join up with the positions gained by the 7th Division through the western part of the Quarries to the Cité St. Elie.

"Every care must be taken throughout the attack to maintain touch with the neighbouring units. At the same time, no leader is justified in delaying his advance in order to keep pace with a unit on his flanks." [F.S.R.]

The 7th Division was able to push on over a mile east of the Fosse 8, where the troops on their northern flank were fighting, and later they gained touch with these troops, although the Germans were not cleared out of their trenches between the Quarries and St. Elie. Farther south, where the 1st, 15th, and 47th Divisions were fighting, the advance was carried even farther into the German defences than was the case on the front of the I Corps.

During the first hour of the attack on the left of this Corps, two brigades reached the outskirts of Hulluch village, and, though the right attacking brigade of the 1st Division was temporarily held up by barbed-wire entanglements south of Lone Tree, the 15th Division was able to advance farther east, and within one and a half hours its left attacking brigade had captured Chalk Pit, Puits 14 bis, Hill 70, and the western edge of the village of Cité St. Elie, while its right brigade was assaulting Loos from the north.

At Loos, the division on the right of our First Army was able to co-operate with the southern brigade of the 15th Division after driving the enemy from the slag-heap called Double Crassier, and after crossing the Bethune-Lens Road. This division carried out the principle of advancing irrespective of the progress on the flank.

The French Tenth Army did not start their attack till 1225 hours, and then their nearest troops were nearly five miles from where our right-flank troops were fighting in the vicinity of Loos. This made the progress of our southern flank necessarily precarious. The result of our operations by 1300 hours was favourable for a counter-attack from the enemy's point of view.

Our division north of the Vermelles-Hulluch Road was in a difficult position in the triangle St. Elie-Haisnes-Hulluch

Quarries; the brigades engaged round Fosse 8 and at Hohenzollern Redoubt were unable to progress; our northern flank of the I Corps could not advance south of the Bethune-La Bassée Canal. The Germans also had brought unexpectedly strong forces to check the French, who were advancing towards Souchez and the Vimy Heights.

The Crown Prince of Bavaria, in his counter-attack, was able to concentrate superior numbers against our troops at Hill 70, Puits 14 bis, and in the houses on the western edge of Cité St. Auguste. There had been no time for our troops to consolidate their positions, and the enemy had heavy artillery with which to support their attack closely.

The result of the counter-attack was that the houses in Cité St. Auguste and most of Hill 70 were, before dark, again in the enemy's possession.

With reference to the employment of reserves, the following from F.S.R. is applicable: "The siting and movement of the reserves require careful consideration."

In this operation, our reserves consisted of the XI Corps and the 3rd Cavalry Division. Two of the divisions of the XI Corps on the night before the attack were in the vicinity of Beuvry, Noeux-les-Mines, and Lillers, ten miles northwest of Bethune. Our division at Bailleul could be sent to any point north or south of the La Bassée Canal, so that the Crown Prince of Bavaria, commanding the German forces on our front, could not foresee where they might be required in the coming operations.

It was hoped that, if the German lines were pierced by the action of our artillery and infantry, the cavalry from the area west of our IV Corps could get through the gap made into the plain beyond the Hulluch-Loos-Vimy Height.

Our Regulations also state that:—

" As the attack progresses the reserves should be moved forward, preferably by bounds, so that they may be able to reinforce or relieve units in the front line, or to exploit success without delay. On the other hand, reserves should not be moved so far forward that they suffer severe losses, become involved in local fighting, or lose their power of movement, and thus become unable to take advantage of a good opening or to deal with counter-attacks."

In this case, when, at 0930 hours, we had captured Loos and the 15th Division were in the western outskirts of Cité St. Auguste, two of the reserve divisions were placed at the disposal of the First Army Commander. They were then about three hours' march from our present forward positions.

The First Army Commander immediately ordered his reserves up to the support of the attacking troops.

By 1130 hours, the heads of both these divisions were within one hour's march of the original starting line. The German counter-attacks by the Prussian Guard and by the 15th Bavarian Division were able to materialize before our reserve divisions could give effective assistance in exploiting success. By nightfall, our first objective had not been reached, and we were holding from the Double Crassier with our right flank to the south of Loos and the western edges of Hill 70 and round Chalk Pit Wood. There was then a gap of 1,300 yards to Alley A, where our line ran up east of Corons, including Hohenzollern Redoubt, and then north-west along our original line.

In many places, the Germans were still holding trenches in the gaps in their positions, and nearly a sixth of our forces had become casualties. Thus the difficulty of carrying out the principles for the use of reserves, as laid down in F.S.R., is apparent. The difficulty of their use lies in the choice between having the reserves so far forward that they become too early involved in the fighting, or having them in a position too far back, from which they cannot exploit success without delay.

In view of our present knowledge, we can say that, if the First Army Commander had had three divisions available to exploit the successes at Loos, west of Hulluch and Cité St. Elie and towards Haisnes, as gained by four of his divisions, our initial dashing attack and the surprise from which the enemy suffered might have led to a substantial gain of ground. As it was, the divisional reserves were used up in the course of the day's fighting, and the Germans were able to bring up reinforcements and reserves, whose counter-attacks caused us heavy losses and enabled them to regain ground east of Loos, at Puits 14 bis, and at the Quarries.

We are told that: " Before any portion of the general reserves are thrown in to take the place of leading units or formations, the commander must be assured that success cannot be achieved without such action."

" To enable a commander to employ his reserves to the best advantage he must keep in close touch with the situation." In the Despatches of October 15th, 1915, it is stated that, between 1100 and 1200 hours on September 25th, the central brigades of the 21st and 24th Divisions filed past the Commander-in-Chief at Bethune and Noeux-les-Mines respectively. By noon, the 44th and 46th Brigades were fighting hard east of Loos and between Lens and Chalet Wood, 4,000 yards from their starting line; the 1st and 2nd Brigades were west of Hulluch, 2,000 yards from their starting line, the 26th and 27th Brigades were west of Haisnes, 2,000 yards from their starting line.

Bethune is six miles from this starting line, so that there was not at this time the close touch advocated in F.S.R. between a commander and his fighting troops. The result was that, as the divisional reserves had been used up and the general reserves were not at hand " to reinforce success," at nightfall the German second line was still intact west of Lens, Cité St. Auguste, Hulluch, Cité St. Elie, Haisnes and La Bassée, and they still held a considerable part of their original front line west of Auchy.

The German use of their reserves seems to have been, from their point of view, satisfactory.

" An immediate counter-attack may succeed in restoring the situation and inflicting heavy casualties on the attacking troops.

" In a counter-attack of this kind the objective will usually be to secure some definite tactical locality, which the enemy has captured, and from which he must be ejected with the least possible delay. If the counter-attack is to be successful it must be delivered with rapidity and precision by troops already on the spot and specially detailed for an emergency of this nature." [F.S.R. 82 (2).]

From the Germans' point of view, when our attacks had reached their limit on September 25th, and when they realized that the French attacks in Champagne and on our southern flank near Souchez did not necessitate the expenditure of their reserves in those areas, the time was favourable for counter-attacks; especially as we had not been able to break through their second line and there were many gaps between the positions which we had won.

During the night September 25th/26th, the Germans made frequent counter-attacks with their reserves, and we were forced to give way at the Quarries and Fosse Alley. Our reserves were not in a position to give effective support, as the bulk of the general reserve had been on the move during the night, in order to reach positions about the Grenay-Hulluch Road and the Loos-Haisnes Road. Their difficulty was that the road-control in rear of our battle area had not been arranged for the march of reinforcements to our forward areas, but for the evacuation of casualties, and for the necessary refilling, meeting and delivery points for ammunition and supplies.

The result was that, by dawn on September 26th, two battalions of one of our reserve divisions were in support of our forward line of trenches on the western slope of Hill 70, one brigade had taken over positions at and north of the Chalk Pit, with one brigade in support north of Loos. The other reserve division was assembled in our original trenches west of Hohenzollern Redoubt by 1900 hours, and by 0100 hours one of its brigades occupied our forward positions from Fosse 8 down to Fosse Alley, connecting up with our troops on their left in the old German line.

The difficulties of making a plan for September 26th were considerable, owing to the following factors. The effect of surprise would no longer be possible. Our subsidiary attack and the naval and the Belgian demonstration on the coast had not held off or prevented the enemy from sending reserves to our front. The Germans in our front still had a strong line, and, therefore, our advance would be costly and precarious. We had learnt at Neuve Chapelle that we had been able in a first attack to gain our immediate objective, but that subsequent attacks, in which the German reserves had time to take a part, caused us a loss of approximately 10,000 men, and no further gain of ground.

When we had made our original attack at zero hour, we had a superiority in numbers and in guns and available ammunition. We had seven times as many men in our six divisions as the enemy had on our front. We had twice as many heavy guns and four times as many field guns and howitzers as were available to support the Germans between Loos and La Bassée. We had been able to precede our original assault with an hour's bombardment of the German defences, allotting a hundred rounds per field gun and sixty rounds per field and per medium howitzer.

By dawn on September 26th, we had had approximately 15,500 casualties, our guns and ammunition had been depleted, and the enemy had been considerably reinforced. Two of our reinforcing divisions were very tired after the fatiguing night operations, and the third division available as a reserve was not at hand to take part in the fighting at dawn, and was not allotted to the First Army until noon on September 26th.

Our offensive operations in May of this year cost us heavy casualties after our first gains, as we did not consolidate them strongly and wait for further reinforcements of personnel, artillery and ammunition before continuing the attacks.

The conclusion from these battles then appeared to be that, after the initial attack, unless we had made a gap through the German defences or unless the whole German front was attacked or menaced, the subsequent advance would, on a narrow front, lead, as before, to the Germans massing reserves against a threatened part and causing further successes to be bought at an excessive loss in men and material from concentrated artillery fire on a narrow front. A general offensive could, on the other hand, only be carried out when we had accumulated a great superiority of men, guns and ammunition. Without this superiority in artillery, our losses must be heavy, in view of the strength of the enemy's positions. In this case, if we did advance on our front, we should add to the salient between our troops and the French Tenth Army on our right. The French Tenth Army south of Lens was now three miles west of our forward positions. Therefore, if they were not able to advance, a considerable part of our striking force—at least two divisions—would be required to join up our line with theirs. On the 25th, the French had been unable to capture Vimy Ridge.

This was, however, only considering our own point of view, and the original instructions given to the First Army Commander must be borne in mind. These were to co-operate with all possible strength and vigour in the French operations.

As indicated in our Field Service Regulations, the question of policy in framing a plan must always be considered, and in this case it was the deciding factor. Orders were consequently issued for a further offensive operation to be carried out on our three-mile front from Hill 70 to half a mile northwest of Hulluch.

In F.S.R. is the following paragraph, which is applicable to the orders issued for September 26th:—

"Under all conditions the attacking troops must be given definite objectives by their immediate commanders and the principle must be remembered that higher commanders allot tasks, and leave the method of carrying them out to their subordinates, subject always to coordination by the former."

Our limit of exploitation was to be the line of the Haute Deule Canal. The definite objectives allotted to divisions were Hill 70, Hulluch, and Cité St. Elie.

On the morning of September 26th, there was a thick mist, making accurate observation of artillery fire and consequently the support of the infantry attacks matters of difficulty. The redoubt on Hill 70 and the positions on either side of it had been considerably strengthened; units were much scattered and mixed up during the night, and it was not easy to get orders through to all in the time available before the attack started. Our maps were on a small scale, and our supporting battalions in the initial attack at 0900 hours advanced towards Loos Crassier instead of against the objective. Our Regulations state that:—

"As a general guide, orders for a deliberate attack should reach infantry brigade headquarters not less than 48 hours before zero hour."

In this case, it was not possible to do this, but the adequate time not being available for the executive commanders to deal with their allotted tasks, militated against the success of the operation.

F.S.R. states:—

"On receipt of his allotted tasks, a subordinate commander will at once carry out the necessary reconnaissances and form his own plan. He will in turn hold a conference of his subordinates at which the rôle of his own command and of corresponding commands on either flank will be described, his intentions explained and subordinate tasks distributed."

To carry out these preliminary arrangements was not possible, as orders for the attack on Hill 70 did not reach battalion commanders until an hour before the artillery bombardment was due to begin, and in some cases companies did not receive them until after it had begun. In spite of much gallantry, we were unable to gain a position farther forward than the western side of Hill 70 below its crest, and to join up through the Loos Crassier with the left of the 47th Division south of Loos.

The difficulty of our Corps attacking the centre of the German position between Bois Hugo and Hulluch was that they would be outflanked if the troops north and south of them were unable to capture Hulluch, the Bois, and Hill 70.

In addition, the advance of this central Corps would have to be across the open for 1,000 yards against an unbroken line held by six battalions protected by strong, thick, wire entanglements. Nor was it possible to have the "sustained and overwhelming covering fire throughout the attack," as advocated in F.S.R. before the delivery of a deliberate attack; nor was it possible to have a preliminary gas attack.

All the attacking troops were very tired, and only one brigade had a hot meal before starting. Our difficulties were further increased by the enemy's counter-attacks from Hulluch, Cité St. Auguste, and Bois Hugo, so that there was considerable disorganization and loss in repelling them before the main attack started.

The advance of the two reserve divisions of the XI Corps was not synchronized, for its southern division was giving ground in front of the German attacks when the leading brigade of its northern division began to advance, so that "the maximum co-operation between all arms and a full development of artillery fire," as F.S.R. point out are most desirable, were not possible.

"Surprise is the most effective and powerful weapon in war." This weapon we could have no chance of using on September 26th, as our offensive was not timed to start until 1100 hours. The steady advance of the leading brigade of the northern division raised the *morale* of the somewhat disorganized troops, who had been endeavouring to deal with the German counter-attacks, and enabled them to turn again and join in the attack, but they could not give complete co-operation.

F.S.R. states that:—

"Co-operation can be maintained during a battle only if close personal touch exists between the commanders of the various arms engaged. This cannot be ensured unless the principles with regard to liaison and the position of commanders in the field are clearly established and followed."

This was not possible, owing to the short time available for preparation and the lack of information as to our objective and the route to it, and owing to the enemy's counter-attacks. In addition to the attackers on the southern flank of the XI Corps not being able to reach the redoubt on Hill 70, there was a similar failure to capture Hulluch on the northern flank, so that at the end of our day's fighting our position from Hill 70 turned back to the north-west up to the Loos-La Bassée Road, which it followed for 1,000 yards, running then in a north-easterly direction to within 600 yards of Hulluch. Beyond this point, our position was unchanged.

"An army depends for success on the combined efforts of its component parts." [F.S.R.]

Such a combination as is considered necessary for success was rendered difficult for the division detailed to capture Hulluch.

Owing to conflicting reports reaching divisional headquarters as to the situation on their right flank, and owing to the attack by the southern division of the I Corps on Cité St. Elie being delayed, the attack on Hulluch was postponed until midday, the fire of the guns was brought back from their first lift and put on to Hulluch up to the time of the fresh zero hour.

The Brigade Commander attacking west of Bois Carré, however, did not receive the orders postponing the attack until seventy minutes after he had begun his attack in accordance with his original instructions. Another brigade advancing at 1200 hours made an isolated attack against the western side of Hulluch.

This attack was brought to a standstill by the heavy machine-gun fire of the Germans in the houses of the village, and so the whole assault failed, owing to lack of co-operation. During the morning, the Germans strengthened their main position and their position in Bois Hugo and Chalet Wood. Thus any attack due east north of these woods would be enfiladed at short range before reaching the formidable German second position, in front of which the wire was intact.

The continued advance of the men of the XI Corps consequently caused them to suffer heavily from effective rifle and machine-gun fire at close range from the edge of these two woods, as well as from artillery fire at point-blank range from Hulluch. In spite of their losses from this fire, the advance on the right of the Corps was continued south-east through Chalk Pit Wood and Puits 14 bis.

Here, owing to casualties and lack of a definite objective, the advance came to a standstill, and the attacking troops withdrew back across the Loos-Hulluch Road to the Grenay-Hulluch Road, where two support battalions were. Even the attacks of these two support battalions were without cohesion and without definite objectives, nor did they receive instructions as to the limit of their exploitation. Their commanders at the time of their advance were at brigade headquarters, and so were not able to control their advance, which was carried up to the Lens-La Bassée Road before they also retreated back to their position west of the Grenay-Hulluch Road.

The leading battalions of the 21st Division advanced steadily until they, too, came under most effective enfilade fire from Bois Hugo, and later, when east of the Lens-La Bassée Road, also from Hulluch. Then some troops managed to advance east, others went north-east, where they entered some empty German trenches west of Puits 13 bis, while another battalion advanced south-east.

Large gaps were now formed in our line, which was advancing towards the enemy's second-line trenches and entanglements. The survivors of two and a half battalions managed to crawl up to within fifty yards of the enemy's wire, to find that it had not been cut by our artillery fire. This was the farthest extent of our advance.

All efforts to advance led to immediate casualties, nor were there any troops at hand to take advantage of the success of our troops, who had gained an entrance into the enemy's trenches south of Hulluch. Consequently, these troops withdrew when they saw the general retirement, about 1400 hours.

Our Regulations are definite on this point of supporting a successful action. F.S.R. states that:—

"The greatest pressure should be brought to bear on the enemy by supporting troops in places where the attack is progressing rather than where it is held up. Every effort should be made to increase the gap caused by the successful penetration at one point of the enemy's position."

At 1400 hours on this day (September 26th), the nearest Guards Brigade was clear of Noeux-les-Mines on the road to Vermelles, five and a half miles from Hulluch. It was not till sunset that two of the Guards Brigades reached the La Bassée-Vermelles railway line, three miles west of Hulluch, so that immediate pressure or any exploitation by these supporting troops was not possible till after dark. Their rate of progress was due to the difficulties of road control and the consequent congestion of traffic.

The withdrawal of the bulk of the 21st and 24th Divisions was covered by about 500 men, who remained in the positions which they had reached close to the enemy's wire entanglements, so that the Germans did not follow up our retreat, which was checked by 1500 hours in the vicinity of the German original trench line, about 1,500 yards west of Loos, and 2,500 yards west of Hulluch.

Farther south, owing to a misunderstanding, there was much confusion and a general retirement from Hill 70 by the troops who had been holding its western slope. Possibly this difficulty could have been adjusted by the divisional headquarters had they been in the vicinity. F.S.R. lays down that:—

"The headquarters of divisions and of lower formations should be so placed as to enable the commander to keep in close and constant touch with his fighting troops, with his reserves, and with the other arms supporting him, and, if necessary, to intervene personally in the conduct of the battle. The headquarters of an attacking unit must be established well forward from the beginning of the battle, and must be moved forward by bounds in order to keep touch with the troops as they advance. Good means of intercommunication are necessary for the successful direction of operations."

In this case, an unsigned order to retire was acted on by the commander of the most forward troops on Hill 70, in spite of the fact that at the time the Germans were inactive. The situation on our southern flank was finally adjusted by the

3rd Cavalry and Guards Divisions taking up positions to cover Loos. The Germans advanced only to the Lens-La Bassée Road. Farther north, although we were unable to recapture the Quarries during the afternoon of the 26th, owing to the fact that our advance was across open ground swept by shell and heavy machine-gun fire, and that there was no surprise after the two hours' bombardment of our objective, and that our troops came on to the unexpected obstacle of the very deep original German trenches, where the enemy bombers were active, a position was gained by the force specially detailed for this enterprise astride the Loos-La Bassée Road, joining up with the troops on their northern flank.

On our southern flank, the French had been able to make little progress. The nearest part of their Tenth Army to our flank was three miles away. It had been able to advance half a mile.

On the following day, September 27th, the brigade holding Fosse 8 was unable to maintain its position there, and it was slowly forced back by a converging attack of enemy bombers, who followed up an intense bombardment on the trenches between this post and the Hohenzollern Redoubt. The difficulty of holding our position was owing to the salient formed at the Dump, where our lines joined and then ran east and south.

In this connection, our Regulations state that " almost every position has its salients, which constitute a weakness owing to the facility with which converging fire can be brought to bear on them."

A new line was, therefore, established along the eastern face of the Hohenzollern Redoubt. Owing to this withdrawal west of Fosse 8, the situation of the troops farther south in Fosse Alley became untenable, as again the German bombers were able to make their converging attacks down empty trenches, covered by accurate artillery and machine-gun fire. We had to readjust our positions in this area and retire back to the line of the original German trenches. Our attempt to recapture the Dump during the night September 27th/28th was vigorously carried forward to within 70 yards of the enemy's position at the Fosse and up to the Dump, but they could not capture the enemy's position, owing to the fact that there was no surprise, the enemy being able to observe our advance in the bright moonlight.

The rest of the action on September 27th concerns the advance of the Guards Division south of the Hulluch Road. The 9th and 15th Divisions were to become the general reserves at Bethune and Noeux-les-Mines respectively.

The redoubt on Hill 70 was to be taken during the afternoon

by a simultaneous attack from the north and west by two brigades, while another brigade secured the line of the Lens-La Bassée Road farther north.

"It is essential that arrangements should be made to ensure that attacks intended to be simultaneous are so in reality. This requires close co-operation between the commanders concerned and co-ordination by the higher formation."

This principle, laid down in F.S.R., was carefully carried out in our attacks on September 27th.

"Whether in attack or defence the first thought of a commander must be to outwit his adversary. [F.S.R.]

This was done by distracting the enemy's attention from the main point of attack by a renewed attempt to recapture the Chalk Pit Copse and a discharge of gas in our sector north-west of Auchy. At 1600 hours, after heavy artillery bombardment, our operations began. The objectives and frontages had been carefully allotted to units, and the situation had throughout been clearly defined.

In the central brigade, the objectives, after the crossing of the Loos-Hulluch Road, were the Chalk Pit at the northern end of a spinney, and Puits 14 bis south of it. Two battalions were to capture the Chalk Pit, then one battalion was to advance and capture Puits 14 bis.

One battalion was to remain in reserve.

"Special importance attaches to the suitable siting of the reserves in order that the commander may be ready to deal with new developments in the situation." [F.S.R.]

The Chalk Pit Wood and Chalk Pit were captured at the first assault, as the enemy had not been able to observe our advance.

But the capture of Puits 14 bis was difficult, as the advancing battalion was exposed to heavy machine-gun fire at less than 2,000 yards' range from Bois Hugo. However, they were able to capture the Puits buildings and to establish a line an hour and a half later on the eastern edge of the Chalk Pit. The brigade advancing against Hill 70 came under heavy artillery fire from the northern suburbs of Lens as soon as they crossed the ridge west of Loos.

Battalions then advanced steadily in artillery formation to the lower slopes of Hill 70, where they were immune from any heavy bombardment. It was not until they gained the crest of this hill that they again were under heavy fire, and they were then forced to take up a position 100 yards west of the crest. Here they gained touch with the dismounted 3rd Cavalry Division on their right.

F.S.R. states that:—

"It is only in the last resort that cavalry should be dismounted to take part in the fighting during position warfare. The separation of cavalry formations from their horses, and their employment as weak bodies of infantry, lead to the loss of opportunities for mounted action at a time when their mobility as a mounted reserve may be of the greatest value."

This was an occasion when it was necessary to use cavalry dismounted. Our Commander-in-Chief had informed the French Commander that he would be forced to stop his offensive unless the French Tenth Army Commander could relieve the situation on his right flank with a rapid and vigorous attack, as our right flank was exposed and our reserves were being rapidly exhausted.

Our division on our southern flank had been able to advance and to capture and hold Chalk Pit Wood east of Loos, in spite of the German counter-attacks. The division on the northern sector of our front had not been effective, owing to the wind being unsuitable for a gas attack in an easterly direction.

On September 28th, arrangements were made for a reduction of our frontage before we continued to advance and attack the German second position preparatory to our attempt to reach our original objective, the Haute Deule Canal, farther east. The difficulty of the situation for a renewed offensive was that the factor of surprise was no longer in our favour.

We had failed to gain our original objective when it was possible to surprise the enemy, when we had superior numbers on our front of attack, and when we had three divisions as a general reserve available to exploit success before the enemy, who were being attacked in Champagne by three French armies, and in Artois by the French Tenth Army, could know where to send their reserves.

Our casualties had been heavy, and the *morale* of the enemy had not been unduly lowered by the loss of parts of their first line.

However, in order to co-operate with the French, our attacks were continued on the 28th. The French were to take over Hill 70 and Loos, and our First Army was to press on through the German second position east of Cité St. Laurent, towards Pont à Vendin and towards Wingles.

Our main operation on September 28th was to capture Puits 14 bis on the northern side of Hill 70, as from it the

Germans could enfilade our whole position east of Loos. Unfortunately, however, when our leading companies advanced at 1600 hours for the capture of their objective, it was found that the artillery had not been able to locate the enemy's gun position in Bois Hugo, so that of the attacking battalion only small parties managed to reach the Puits. We had to fall back again to the Chalk Pit and the Wood south of it in touch with the dismounted cavalry. Puits 14 bis now remained in "No Man's Land."

The French Army on our right flank was able to make progress on September 28th against the enemy's third line on Vimy Ridge.

On the last day of September, the Commander-in-Chief issued a special Order of the Day:—

"We have now reached a definite stage in the great battle which commenced on the 23rd inst. Our Allies in the south have pierced the enemy's last line of entrenchments and effected large captures of prisoners and guns.

"The Tenth French Army, on our immediate right, has been heavily opposed, but has brilliantly succeeded in securing the important position known as Vimy Ridge. The operations of the British forces have been most successful, and have had great and important results. On the morning of the 25th inst., the First and Fourth Corps attacked and carried the enemy's first and most powerful line of entrenchments, extending from our extreme right flank at Grenay to a point north of the Hohenzollern Redoubt—a distance of 6,500 yards. The position was exceptionally strong, consisting of a double line, which included some large redoubts and a network of trenches and bomb-proof shelters.

"Dug-outs were constructed at short intervals all along the line, some of them being large caves 30 ft. below the ground. The Eleventh Corps in general reserve and the Third Cavalry Division were subsequently thrown into the fight and finally the 28th Division. After the vicissitudes attendant upon every great fight, the enemy's second line posts were taken, the commanding position known as Hill 70, in advance of Loos, was finally captured, and a strong line was established and consolidated in close proximity to the German third and last line.

"The main operations south of the La Bassée Canal, were much facilitated and assisted by the subsidiary attacks delivered by the Third and Indian Corps, and the troops of the Second Army. Great help was also rendered by the operations of the Fifth Corps east of Ypres, during which some important captures were made. Our captures have amounted to over 3,000 prisoners and some 25 guns, besides many machine guns and a quantity of war material. The enemy has suffered heavy losses, particularly in the many counter-attacks by which he has vainly endeavoured to wrest back the captured positions, but which have all been gallantly repulsed by our troops."

There was now a lull in the operations, in order to prepare for our fresh offensive, which it was agreed should commence on October 6th. A fresh starting line was constructed west of and parallel to the Lens-La Bassée Road. Our difficulties in preparing for a further offensive were considerable, owing to the dominating positions which the enemy occupied on Hill 70 and on the Dump, from which they could overlook our positions in the vicinity of these posts.

To add to our difficulties, the Germans concentrated superior numbers in a converging attack on the Hohenzollern Redoubt from both sides of the Dump on the night of October 2nd/3rd, at a time when a relief was taking place. They were successful in capturing this redoubt.

It was then decided to concentrate all available men, guns and gas for its recapture, and for an attack on Fosse 8 and the Quarries. This concentration, however, was delayed for a considerable time, as it was necessary to bring up and instal gas cylinders and to construct fresh trenches as starting lines and also communication trenches leading up to them.

The result was that the main attack in co-operation with the French would have to be postponed. This time of preparation gave the enemy the opportunity of bringing up troops for a counter-attack, in accordance with F.S.R. :—

"The employment of reserve formations for a deliberate counter-offensive will furnish the best means of defeating the enemy, or arresting his further progress in other parts of the battle."

The German counter-attack, which started with a heavy four hours' bombardment at noon on October 8th, was an attempt to recapture the ground they lost between Loos and the La Bassée Canal on September 25th. Their main efforts on our front were bombing attacks made from Fosse 8 and from the Quarries by two divisions.

Our troops, however, were not surprised and held their ground; any temporary successes of the enemy were met by immediate counter-attacks, which succeeded in restoring the situation. As advocated in F.S.R., these counter-attacks were delivered with rapidity and precision by the troops on the spot, to secure a definite tactical locality such as, in this case, the Big Willie Trench, which the enemy captured, and from which he had to be ejected with the least possible delay.

The result of the afternoon's fighting was that the German attacks were definitely repulsed before dark on October 8th. The preparations for our offensive, to be carried out on October 13th, could, therefore, be now continued, but they had been considerably delayed.

Our new plan was to carry out a simultaneous offensive operation with the French Tenth Army against the German salient in our front. Our First Army was to attack on a frontage of three miles in the direction of Loison and Pont à Vendin, and also to improve our position on Hill 70 and at Double Crassier. The French were to co-operate by advancing also on a three-mile front towards Mericourt and Avion, after they had attacked Vimy Ridge.

Before our attack on October 13th, the enemy's trench which was west of our Big Willie Trench, and, in consequence, enfiladed our positions, was captured on October 11th, and it was held in spite of heavy bombardments and determined assaults by the enemy on October 12th.

Our attack on October 13th was preceded by a two hours' continuous bombardment from 445 guns and howitzers of different calibres, in accordance with F.S.R.:—

> "A barrage should normally be organised in several belts of fire so as to give the necessary depth. The fire of the greater portion of the available field guns will form the belt nearest to the infantry, successive belts being formed by the remaining field guns and the field howitzers, by medium howitzers, and by heavy howitzers and some medium guns. Special attention should be paid to the localities from which flanking fire can be brought to bear. The plan of attack will include the allotment of the artillery resources to the various tasks of bombardment, harassing fire, counter-battery work, barrage fire and close support at various stages of the artillery preparation and of the attack."

Our first attack, at 1400 hours on October 13th, started against a definite objective on a 1,400-yard front, to advance our trenches 300 yards into line with those held west of the Lens-La Bassée Road.

Our advance, though resolutely carried out, was checked by the enemy's bombers, and by their enfilade fire from both flanks when our troops reached the wire of the second-line trenches, as our bombardment had not been able to cut more than four gaps in it. These gaps became defiles and death-traps in front of the enemy's machine guns in their trenches a few yards away.

Farther north, one brigade was able to rush across 150 yards of open ground and to capture 200 yards of Gun Trench. The attempt of two other battalions of this brigade to capture the trenches south of the Quarries across 250 yards of open ground was unsuccessful, owing to heavy casualties from machine-gun fire at very close range on their front and flanks. The attack by a brigade farther north against the Quarries was successful in gaining about 300 yards of trench at the south-western corner of this position at heavy cost.

The division on the north had for its first objective the Hohenzollern Redoubt and Fosse 8. The difficulties in making this attack were increased by the short time at the disposal of commanders for gaining information about the position to be attacked, as the troops had not reached their positions in the trenches from which they were to start the assault until 0600 hours on October 13th.

F.S.R., in this connection, state that:—

"Every commander should obtain by personal reconnaissance as thorough a grasp as time will allow of the ground over which his troops may become engaged and the topographical difficulties which they may encounter. The smaller the formation or unit the more detailed must this reconnaissance be."

In our first assault, which started at 1400 hours, however, two of our attacking battalions reached the Fosse Trench, but, owing to heavy casualties from frontal and flanking machine-gun fire, only small detachments were able to get into the German trench on their front.

Machine guns then were brought up, and, under cover of their fire on the west side of the Hohenzollern Redoubt, positions were consolidated by a fresh supporting battalion. The troops in the more forward Fosse Trench withdrew during the night back to the redoubt. Our most northerly division endeavoured to capture the Little Willie Trench, but without success.

The shortage of hand grenades led to heavy casualties among our bombers, who gained a little ground up North Face and up the Little Willie Trenches. Fighting continued in the trenches in and near the redoubt until the 15th. On October 19th, the Commander-in-Chief was able to report that we had made the following gain of ground:—

"The new front now leaves our old line at a point about 1,200 yards south-west of the southern edge of the

Auchy-lez-La Bassée Road and runs thence, through the main trench of the Hohenzollern Redoubt, in an easterly direction, 400 yards south of the northern buildings of Fosse 8 to the south-west corner of the Quarries.

"We also hold the south-eastern corner of the Quarries, our trenches running thence south-east parallel to and 400 yards from the south-western edge of Cité St. Elie to a point 500 yards west of the north edge of Hulluch.

"The line then runs along the Lens-La Bassée Road to the Chalk Pit, 1,500 yards north of the highest point of Hill 70, and then turns south-west to a point 1,000 yards east of Loos Church, where it bends south-east to the north-west slope of Hill 70 and runs along the western slopes of that hill, bending south-west to a point 1,300 yards south of Loos Church, whence it runs due west back to our old line. The chord of the salient we have created in the enemy's line measured along our old front is 700 yards in length, the depth of the salient at the Chalk Pit is 3,200 yards."

CHAPTER V.

DIARY OF EVENTS.

1915.

April 6th.—General Joffre issued his plan for offensive operations in which the French Tenth Army and the British First Army would co-operate on a front of approximately twenty miles, from the north of Arras to the vicinity of Fromelles. This operation was to be a part of the general offensive on the whole front from (1) Verdun and Nancy in a northerly direction; (2) from Reims in a north-easterly direction; (3) in an easterly direction from Artois.

The First Army of the B.E.F. on the north of the French Tenth Army was to attack in a south-easterly direction towards La Bassée and Aubers Ridge, in order to reach La Bassée and Fournes.

April 9th.—Further details of our plan were arranged. The B.E.F. would have for the intended operation ten divisions, 637 guns and howitzers, and five cavalry divisions in reserve.

April 17th.—The Second Army's fight began for Hill 60, south-east of Ypres.

April 22nd.—The Commander-in-Chief acknowledged the feats performed by the Second Army at Hill 60, as follows:—

" I congratulate you and the troops of the Second Army on your brilliant capture and retention of the important position of Hill 60."

The Germans followed their bombardment of the trenches between Bixschoote and Langemarck with a gas attack upon the French and Canadians. They gained a few miles of ground. For the next ten days, there was heavy fighting to re-establish the line east of Ypres.

April 23rd.—Troops from our 27th and 28th Divisions and 13th Brigade pushed forward east of Ypres.

April 28th.—We held our positions. The French advanced. The fighting in this Second Battle of Ypres lasted until the end of May, and, though the Germans gained some ground, they failed to reach their final objective.

May 1st.—Mackensen's Third and Fourth Armies began operations on a fifty-mile front against the Russian line between Gorlice and Tarnow.

May 4th.—Orders were issued for the First Army to take the offensive on May 8th.

May 6th.—The main plan for the offensive of the First Army was issued, namely, for a general offensive to be undertaken by the I, Indian, and IV Corps on a front between Rue du Marais to Ver Touquet. Our advance was then to be continued to the Haute Deule Canal between Bauvin and Don.

May 7th.—Orders were sent to postpone the main attack and the arrival of troops in their assembly positions.

May 9th.—Battle of Aubers Ridge.

Our troops consisted of: —

I Corps.—1st, 2nd and 47th Divisions.
IV Corps.—7th, 8th and 49th Divisions.
Indian Corps.—51st, Lahore and Meerut Divisions.
Three squadrons, Royal Flying Corps.
In Army reserve were five cavalry divisions, the Canadian, 50th, and 51st Divisions.

Opposed to the First Army Corps were ten German regiments.

0230 hours: Troops of the IV Corps were in their assembly position. The 8th Division had the 24th and 25th Brigades as forward brigades, each on a front of 750 yards, north-west of Rouges Bancs (3½ miles north-east of Neuve Chapelle).

The 23rd Brigade was in Divisional reserve. The 7th Division was similarly formed up on a two-brigade front a mile behind the front of the 8th Division. The 49th Division and two battalions of the 21st Brigade formed the Corps reserve.

0500 hours: 373 guns of the IV Corps began to bombard the German trenches, localities and communications. The German counter-batteries and machine guns, however, were not silenced.

0530 hours: The leading companies of the 2nd and 3rd Brigades of the 1st Division formed up in "No Man's Land" for the attack. The frontage to be assaulted by this Division was 1,600 yards in a south-easterly direction towards Ferme du Bois and the Distillery. At the same time north of the 1st Division the Meerut Division on a 800-yard front sent the leading companies of the Dehra Dun Brigade over the parapet, and the front companies also of the 24th and 25th Brigades formed up ready for the assault.

The leading troops of the 1st Division reached the enemy's wire, and the Meerut Division reached a line about half-way to the German first line by 0540 hours.

0540 hours: The general assault started. Two mines under the German trenches were exploded on the 8th Division front. The 1st/13th London Regiment on the left front of the 25th Brigade occupied the crater formed, and the leading companies of the 2nd Rifle Brigade and 1st Royal Irish Rifles on the right of this brigade reached a point 200 yards beyond the German line.

0620 hours: The 25th Brigade reserves were sent to reinforce the forward troops, some of whom began to withdraw at this time. Parties of four battalions, however, remained in the positions which they had reached.

0745 hours: A further hour's bombardment of the enemy's trenches on a front of 3,900 yards was made.

0830 hours: The attack of the IV Corps was brought to a standstill.

0845 hours: Orders were sent to the IV Corps to press their attack vigorously towards Rouges Bancs. Artillery bombardment was, therefore, carried out on the German trenches south of the positions occupied by the Northamptons.

1200 hours was fixed as the time for a new attack to be started by the 1st and Meerut Divisions. Owing to the very heavy losses in both divisions, the reorganization could not take place, so zero hour was postponed till 1600 hours.

In the meantime, the 1st Brigade took the place of the 2nd Brigade for the assault, which was started on the 1st Division front by one battalion at 1557 hours; another battalion of the 1st Brigade started to attack three minutes later with two companies and with the remainder of the battalion at 1640 hours. In our first assault at 1557 hours, the few men who reached the German trenches were killed.

The remaining companies were unable to reach the German trenches, owing to heavy machine-gun fire. On the front of the 3rd Brigade, our men were not able to advance more than 100 yards.

1330 hours: The 24th Brigade, with a battalion of the 7th Division, and the 25th and 23rd Brigades in support, attacked the enemy's trenches. This attack failed.

The 21st Brigade from Army reserve was sent up to the IV Corps for a renewed attempt to take the German trenches This attack was to start after dusk at 2000 hours.

1635 hours: German trenches were bombarded for ten minutes. The attacks on the front of the 1st Division were then abandoned. Those who were lying in " No Man's Land " were able to return to our original trenches after dark.

It was reported from the Meerut Division that further assaults would be useless against the heavy and accurate machine-gun fire of the Germans.

The plan for the IV Corps was to attack in a south-easterly direction and join up on their right with the left of the Indian Corps at La Cliqueterie Farm, 3,500 yards west of the northern end of our front-line trench where it was held by the Jullundur Brigade. The first objective of the 8th Division, which was to attack on a 1,400-yard front, was Fromelles. The 7th Division, its right protected by two battalions and a battery, was then to keep its left on the 8th Division and continue to advance in a south-easterly direction, in order to join up with the Indian Corps.

1800 hours: The order for another attack was cancelled. During the night, efforts were made to reach our detachments in the German lines.

May 10*th.*—0230 hours: Germans made a counter-attack. Two battalions of the 25th Brigade made an effort to reach the 1st/13th London Regiment. Only small parties, however, were able to reach the German trenches.

0300 hours: The Germans had re-established their original front line, and all our detachments returned to their trenches. Our total losses since the First Army attack began were now estimated at 11,600.

0900 hours: The First Army Commander decided to concentrate all available troops, including the 7th Division which had not yet been engaged, for an attack to be delivered south of Neuve Chapelle, in order to co-operate with the French Tenth Army engaged on Vimy Ridge. The French here had heavy hand-to-hand fighting on the ridge up to the 15th, but they were unable to capture the crest of the hill.

Our attacks at Aubers Ridge had not been of great assistance to them, as we had not drawn on to our sector the Army reserves of the Sixth German Army at Roubaix and Tournai. When our attacks ended on the 9th, the Germans were able to send these reserves to the Vimy Ridge battle area.

1320 hours: Orders were issued for the 7th Division to march after dark to the I Corps area north of Festubert.

May 11*th.*—0400 hours: The 7th Division reached positions west of Bethune.

May 12*th*: The French Commander-in-Chief urged on the Commander-in-Chief of the B.E.F. either the necessity for continuing the offensive with the First Army, or that a French division south of the La Bassée Canal should be relieved, so that the French at Vimy could be reinforced, or that two

British divisions should be sent to the French Tenth Army to co-operate with them in their attacks.

Two brigades of the 1st Division occupied the sector south of Givenchy in the place of the 4th Guards Brigade.

May 13th.—Our Commander-in-Chief decided to renew the offensive north of Festubert, and that the infantry assault should start on May 15th after a long, methodical bombardment, and that a division should relieve the French division which was just south of the First Army positions.

Major-General Barter's Force was formed. It consisted of the 1st and 47th Divisions. The thirty-six-hour bombardment of the enemy trenches on a 5,000-yard front began.

May 14th.—Our 1st Division relieved the French 58th Division on a 5,500-yard front just south of the La Bassée Canal. Our 47th Division, less one brigade, occupied the ground vacated by the 1st Division north of the Canal. The 51st Division marched to the Bailleul-Cassel area to act as general reserve.

May 15th.—The Commander-in-Chief sanctioned the following plan for operations to be commenced on May 15th, namely, to prosecute a " deliberate and persistent attack." After a short, intensive bombardment, the 7th Division was to attack at daylight on the 15th on a front of 850 yards, from the north of Festubert in an easterly direction. The 2nd Division was to attack before midnight, May 14th/15th, in a south-easterly direction on a front of 1,300 yards. The left flank of this division was to be supported by the attack of the Garhwal Brigade on a 400-yard front.

The enemy on our immediate front of attack were part of the German VII Corps, approximately 2,200 men. Our total numbers were nearly five times more than those of the enemy at the time of our initial assault.

The first objective for these two divisions was to be the Germans' first-line and support trenches on their front. They were to re-form and join up on the La Quinque Rue after an advance of approximately 1,000 yards. On this line they were to eliminate the 600-yard gap between their inner flanks. Then after a bombardment there was to be a general advance for approximately another 1,000 yards by the two divisions in an easterly direction to the Rue du Marais. The final limit of exploitation was to be on a front of approximately 2,500 yards for a distance of another 1,000 yards, from Rue du Marais to the vicinity of Chapelle St. Roch-Beau Puits. The R.F.C. were to co-operate by bombing German headquarters, observation posts, and the railways running to Lille.

The Canadian Division (less Divisional Artillery) moved to the Busnes-Calonne area to be in reserve. The dispositions before the Battle of Festubert were as follows for the I Corps, who were making the attacks:—

The 7th Infantry Division was on a front of 1,500 yards, from 400 yards south of the Rue des Cailloux to 700 yards west of the western point of the Ferme Cour d'Avoué.

The 22nd and 20th Brigades equally subdivided this front, with the 22nd Brigade in the southern sector, the 20th Brigade in the northern sector, and the 21st Brigade in Divisional reserve.

The 47th and 1st Divisions continued the trench line south of the 7th Division. Six hundred yards north of the 7th Division was the southern flank of the 2nd Division, holding a front of 1,300 yards equally divided between the 6th Brigade in the southern sector and the 5th Brigade in the northern sector.

Their 4th Guards Brigade was in Divisional reserve, about three miles west of the forward trenches.

2330 hours: The assault of the 2nd Division and of the Garhwal Brigade began. The 6th Brigade was successful in reaching the German first-line and support trenches in the first advance. The Germans, however, were more alert farther north in front of the 5th and Garhwal Brigades, and so only one half-battalion which was on the flank of the 6th Brigade was able to get into the German front trench. Nor was it possible to exploit this success.

The French Tenth Army attacked towards Souchez.

May 16th.—0045 hours: Orders were issued for a bombardment of the German trenches to take place at 0245 hours previous to another attack on the northern flank of the 6th Brigade.

0315 hours: The further attacks made by the Lahore and 2nd Divisions failed.

On the front of the 7th Division, the 22nd Brigade attacked on a two-battalion front, each with a frontage of 200 yards on either side of the Rue des Cailloux. The 20th Brigade also attacked on a two-battalion front; each battalion on a 225-yard frontage on either side of the Prince's Road for the attack of the German trenches in their front.

The 1st Royal Welch Fusiliers on the front of the 22nd Brigade reached their objective in the first rush; the other assaulting battalion, the Queen's, after a second bombardment of fifteen minutes, gained the German first line.

The leading battalions of the 20th Brigade carried the first-line trenches in their front at their first assault.

1915 CAMPAIGN IN FRANCE

0600 hours: North Breastwork on the front of the Queen's was taken by this regiment.

0630 hours: The leading troops of the 7th and 2nd Divisions joined up on the road running past the Orchard. The troops fighting near Adalbert Alley, 500 yards north of the Orchard, were forced to give ground and to return to our support trenches.

0900 hours: Our attack was at a standstill. On the front of the 2nd Division, we had been able to hold our positions in the German front-line trenches. The 22nd Brigade had pushed 600 yards beyond the German forward line, and the 6th and 5th Brigades were able to hold the positions which they had won in and just beyond the forward German trenches.

Orders from the I Corps were now sent to the 2nd and 7th Divisions to make further attacks. The 6th Brigade was to advance 1,000 yards in a south-easterly direction from its present position. The 20th Brigade was to try to join up with the 2nd Division on the Rue des Cailloux by attacking in a north-easterly direction.

1000 hours: Our attacks started. Progress was made by the 1st Grenadier Guards of the 20th Brigade for 300 yards up a communication trench leading towards the Quadrilateral, 500 yards south-west of the Ferme Cour d'Avoué.

1430 hours: Our efforts to advance across the open to join up the gap between the 7th and 2nd Divisions were unsuccessful.

The 22nd Brigade on the southern flank of the 7th Division gained a further 800 yards of the general front-line trenches.

1930 hours: Our troops east of La Quinque Rue withdrew to this road, as their forward position had become untenable owing to enfilade fire.

2345 hours: First Army issued orders for offensive operations to be carried out by the I Corps. The gist of these orders was to gain a continuous line along the La Quinque Rue up to the Ferme Cour d'Avoué and then to join up with the original British line by swinging back our left flank in a north-westerly direction along the Cinder Track. The Indian and IV Corps and Barter's Force of two divisions were to stand by and to be ready to co-operate in the general advance, which was to be towards the Chapelle St. Roch-Lorgies Road on the right flank.

The German 5th Regiment failed to regain their lost trenches near Stafford Corner and the Ferme du Bois. Their 11th Jäger Battalion and 104th Regiment were unable to recapture lost trenches west of the Ferme Cour d'Avoué.

May 17th.—During the day, the Germans constructed a new line between the Ferme du Bois and Rue d'Ouvert. This line was occupied by seven battalions.

0245 hours: Our bombardment started. It was mainly directed against the Quadrilateral.

0700 hours: Men from the Saxon regiments in the German forward trenches began to surrender.

The time for our assault was fixed for 0930 hours.

0900 hours: The German forward trenches in the gap between the 7th and 2nd Divisions had been evacuated.

0930 hours: Two battalions of the 21st Brigade advanced towards the Quadrilateral, and in forty-five minutes had occupied it.

1000 hours: The 6th Brigade, owing to the difficulty of getting their orders through to the attacking troops, were thirty minutes late in starting their assault. Their leading troops were able to reach a position 300 yards west of the Ferme Cour d'Avoué.

1130 hours: The I Corps were now ordered to consolidate their front between La Quinque Rue and Cinder Track.

The 3rd Canadian Brigade was attached to the I Corps, whose objective was now to be Chapelle St. Roch and Violaines.

1400 hours: The 7th Division attacked, but was unable to gain ground, owing to heavy enfilade fire. The attack of the 2nd Division was postponed.

1930 hours: The 21st Brigade began their attack in a south-easterly direction towards South Breastwork; 200 men were able to reach this objective, but later had to fall back.

1935 hours: Indian Corps were ordered to continue their attack towards La Quinque Rue as soon as possible on May 18th.

2000 hours: The Guards Brigade reached the front line held by the 21st Brigade.

May 18th.—0300 hours: The further attacks of the 21st Brigade towards South Breastwork were unsuccessful.

0825 hours: The attack was postponed.

1100 hours: The Commander-in-Chief ordered a bombardment to start at 1430 hours, and to be continued for two hours before the attack of the 2nd Canadian and Guards Brigades, who were each to advance on a 650-yard front, from and including both School House and Ferme Cour d'Avoué.

1500 hours: Owing to difficulty in the transmission of orders, our bombardment began at this time.

1630 hours: The Guards Brigade started their advance. Owing to heavy enfilade fire at short range from newly constructed German trenches, the attack had to be discontinued.

1720 hours: The 3rd Canadian Brigade relieved the units of the 21st Brigade in their forward trenches.

1930 hours: The Guards Brigade consolidated positions which they had gained.

May 19th.—The Canadian and 51st Divisions relieved the 7th and 2nd Divisions in the forward trenches between the positions held by the 47th Division and the Indian Corps.

May 20th.—The 1st, 2nd, 7th and 47th Divisions were now the I Corps.

May 23rd.—Italy declared war on Austria.

May 24th.—0230 hours: The 140th and 2nd Canadian Brigades attacked towards South Breastwork. Progress was made.

May 25th.—Artillery bombardment throughout the day was carried out.

1830 hours: The 47th and Canadian Divisions attacked. The 142nd Brigade of the 47th Division advanced 400 yards. The Canadians gained positions 200 yards from the German front lines near South Breastwork. The compensation for our heavy and unavoidable losses was that we had made a general advance of approximately 600 yards on a four-mile front, and we had captured 800 prisoners and 10 machine guns.

The Germans on our front for the operations on this day were fresh troops, namely, a Guards Reserve Brigade, and two other reserve regiments.

May 26th.—Our new positions were consolidated and held. During the past three months, the Germans had gained some ground in the Ypres section of the Allies' line, while we advanced our positions in the vicinity of Festubert and Arras.

There was now a pause, during which the Germans successfully attacked the Russians in co-operation with the Austrians. They were successful in securing the passes of the Carpathians and in driving the Russians out of Poland and across the Vistula; while, in the northern part of our line, there was a series of fights concerned with the capture of trenches near Hooge.

June.—During June, we were advancing up the Euphrates; we were fighting round Krithia and at Gully Ravine in Mesopotamia, and in the Cameroons.

July.—During July, the Italians were fighting on the Isonzo. The Germans in South-West Africa capitulated to General Botha.

August.—During August, our offensive operations in the Dardanelles came to an end after the landing at Suvla on the 6th. By the 10th, on the Italian front, the Isonzo Battle was ended.

September.—In September, our fighting in the Cameroons was continued.

Bulgaria began to mobilize on the 25th.

We agreed with the French to send a force of 150,000 French and British to Salonika. We had now twenty-two divisions on the Western Front, holding from Boesinghe, north of Ypres, to the north of Arras.

The plans for the Battles of Loos, of Artois, and of Champagne were as follows:—

The French were to attack northwards from Champagne west of the Meuse against the German Third Army. The British First Army and the French Tenth Army were to attack from Artois on an eighteen-mile front between Arras and the La Bassée Canal in an easterly direction against the German Sixth Army. The British First Army, consisting of six divisions, with three divisions in general reserve, was to operate on a six-mile front between Grenay and the La Bassée Canal; subsidiary attacks were to be made north of Neuve Chapelle by the III and Indian Corps towards Pietre and Aubers, and by the Second Army, who were between Ypres and Armentières, in the direction of Hooge.

Our general reserve was to consist of the XI Corps and the British and Indian Cavalry Corps. The Indian cavalry were in the vicinity of Doullens. Two British cavalry divisions were posted ten miles north-west of Lillers, and one cavalry division was five miles south-east of this place.

Some of the XI Corps were north and part was south of Lillers. The objective for the cavalry after passing through the infantry and crossing the Haute Deule Canal, five miles east of our front trenches, was to exploit success up to Condé and Tournai and to cut the Lille-Valenciennes railway. The Indian cavalry were to be available to support either the French or British cavalry.

The Royal Flying Corps were to attack the railway line running to Douai, Valenciennes, Courtrai and Lille.

The French were to have seventeen divisions available on their twelve-mile front, from the south of Arras to the south of Loos. Two cavalry divisions were to be ready to exploit their success across the Belgian frontier. In Champagne, the French had thirty-four infantry and nine cavalry divisions available to exploit success towards Sedan and Le Nouvion.

It was hoped that on the whole forty miles of front to be attacked in Champagne and Artois, after an intensive bombardment, the total fifty-seven divisions available for the first assault would carry the two forward lines of German defences.

The First Army was to continue the British offensive with its I and IV Corps of three divisions each, against four German regiments and one Jäger battalion. Our first main assault was to be made by two divisions from each Corps, and by two brigades of the 2nd Division.

Later it was decided that poison gas should be used. This would be effective to a depth of two miles in a favourable wind, and should render ineffective the occupants of the whole forward zone of the enemy's trenches on our whole front of six miles. For this reason, all the six divisions holding our front, from Grenay to astride the La Bassée Canal, were to be engaged.

The German trenches between Loos and Haisnes were to be captured by four divisions, and at the same time our southern division was to form a defensive flank in a south-easterly direction at the Double and Loos Crassiers, while our northern division was to form a defensive flank facing in a north-easterly direction in the vicinity of the La Bassée Canal south of and including both Canteleux and Chapelle St. Roch.

When we had captured the German forward defences, we were to continue our advance to the Haute Deule Canal.

September 21st.—Our four days' preliminary bombardment began on our whole front between Grenay and the La Bassée Canal as soon as it was possible to observe the fire. There were 533 guns and howitzers available for the bombardment of the German wire and of their forward and communication trenches in front of the I and IV Corps.

September 23rd.—The Royal Flying Corps made bombing attacks with thirty-four aeroplanes on the German railway communications near Valenciennes, St. Amand, Wallers and Somain.

September 24th.—The allowance of shells for our artillery bombardment was doubled.

2200 hours: In each of the assaulting divisions, two brigades started to occupy the front trenches. The brigades originally holding the line became Divisional reserves. These reliefs were completed in four and a half hours.

The three general reserve divisions moved into their positions during the night September 24th/25th.

September 25th.—Battle of Loos. In this battle, the following points are brought out that:—

(*a*) The co-operation between the infantry and artillery was not complete.

(*b*) Gas was an unknown factor, and we relied on it to supplement our shortage in artillery and ammunition, which was not sufficient to destroy all the strong points, wire and emplacements on the front on which our six divisions attacked.

(*c*) Lack of experience in intensive artillery preparation led to incomplete results in dealing with hostile machine guns and in destroying the German wire entanglements.

(*d*) Insufficient arrangements were made for consolidation after the capture of important points.

(*e*) Our supplies of grenades were inadequate, so that our bombing attacks to recapture lost positions led to heavy casualties; our loss of Pekin Trench at 1700 hours on the 25th was due to the fact that we had no effective means of replying to the German bombers, who were well supplied with grenades. The German capture of 250 yards of Gun Trench on October 1st was mainly due to their superiority in numbers and quality of bombs.

(*f*) Our reserves were not in positions from which they could exploit success. Considerable results might have been achieved if the First Army Commander's proposal had been carried out, namely, for the 21st and 24th Divisions to have been deployed in rear of Vermelles at daybreak on September 25th. As it was, commanders expected that these divisions would be available to maintain the momentum of the attack and to exploit success when our first objectives had been gained.

Therefore, they used up available troops to gain these objectives.

Our assaulting troops became so weakened in numbers and so much exhausted, that they were unable to push through the German second line, and it was, therefore, vitally important to prevent them from being annihilated by further frontal attacks against strongly entrenched positions. There was, however, delay in bringing up the general reserves, and delay in putting them under the orders of the First Army Commander.

Especially was this the case with the 15th Division,

whose advance up to the defences in front of Cité St. Auguste and with the 7th Division whose advance up to Cité St. Elie had been so successful that the prompt support of the general reserve divisions would have been most valuable, and might have led to decisive results.

(g) The fortifications made since the Battle of Aubers Ridge and the wire put up to guard the German second line were not only very formidable, but they were out of sight and range of our trenches. Our guns were not able to cut the wire effectively or to reduce the *morale* of the defenders; so that only in front of Haisnes and near Cité St. Elie were we able to penetrate into this line.

(h) We did not carry out the principles of exploiting success with local reserves. We made repeated frontal assaults at points where we had been repulsed. This procedure had also proved costly and ineffective at the Battle of Aubers Ridge.

F.S.R. state, in this connection, " every effort should be made to increase the gap caused by the successful penetration at one point of the enemy's position. For this purpose local reserves can be directed against the enemy's flanks."

(i) The collection and transmission of information were so difficult in the forward areas that the commanders in rear gave orders under wrong impressions as to the actual situation of the troops who were in contact with the enemy. For instance, at 1500 hours on September 25th, the First Army Commander " inferred that the First Army was on the crest of the wave of victory; that it had broken through the German second and last line of defence in two central and vital places, Cité St. Elie and Hulluch; and that a break-through at Haisnes and Cité St. Auguste was imminent." (Official History of the War.)

Actually, we had suffered heavy losses; we had not broken through the Germans' second line; we were maintaining our position on Hill 70, west of St. Auguste, with difficulty; and only small parties had crossed the Lens-La Bassée Road.

(j) With reference to leaders and staff, the author of the Official History of the War states: " Troops must be led and there must be leaders in every rank, and in the latter part of 1915 these leaders were in the making. The staff work before and during the battle was very far from perfect. There had been too few staff officers in peace time—two per Regular Division and one per Territorial Division—and only a small reserve. Loos was certainly a difficult battlefield on which to maintain direction from the similarity of the landmarks on it, but the number of occasions on which troops mistook their objectives was extraordinary, *e.g.*, the 15th Division turned south towards Cité St. Laurent instead of going eastwards to Cité St. Auguste; the 21st Division instead of attacking eastwards against Bois Hugo sheered south-east towards Hill 70. It was a difficulty that had been overcome by good staff work at manœuvres in England even in blind country intersected with hedgerows."

0550 hours: On our whole front intensive artillery bombardment and discharge of gas were started. The Germans were surprised by our use of gas, but its effects varied in different parts of the German front according to the wind and the intervening country between our lines.

0630 hours: Our infantry assault began. The artillery shelled the German trenches behind the first line and their communication trenches.

The three brigades of the 2nd Division on the northern flank of the First Army front attacked on a frontage of 3,500 yards. The 5th Brigade was north of the Canal; the 6th and 19th Brigades were south of the Canal.

The 19th Brigade was on the south. This brigade was able to reach the German wire entanglement. This was found to be intact, but, owing to heavy enfilade machine-gun and rifle fire, and as the brigade was without the support of gas and smoke, it was found necessary to withdraw back to the original line. This was done in the course of the day and under cover of darkness by small parties.

The 6th Brigade attacked north of the 19th Brigade up to the La Bassée Canal. The wire on their front was uncut. Our gas cloud incapacitated over a hundred of our own men, and it was so dense that it was difficult to see and to maintain direction. Two mines were exploded under the German trenches. We were able to reach a position east of the mine crater.

North of the Canal, the 5th Brigade was not able to make any progress. The brigade attacked at two places, namely, just north of the Canal with one battalion along the Canal against Tortoise Redoubt, and also with three battalions half a mile farther north. The attack against Tortoise Redoubt was delayed for ten minutes, owing to our own gas being blown across our front trenches, in which the occupants had to be relieved.

When, ten minutes after zero hour, a patrol went forward towards the Tortoise Redoubt, it was overwhelmed by fire, and it was seen that the failure to gain ground south of the Canal would lead to very heavy casualties if the advance was continued in this area. It was, therefore, decided to stand fast.

North of the 5th Brigade, the 58th Brigade attacked at zero hour on a two-battalion front. They were able to advance 200 yards before they were checked. In the course of the morning, they were gradually forced to withdraw to their own front-line trenches.

Farther north, more subsidiary attacks took place on the front of the Indian, III, and V Corps, to distract the enemy's attention from the fighting in the area south of the Canal.

Half an hour before zero, the Garhwal Brigade, of the Meerut Division, attacked towards Pietre. They were checked by the enemy's fire in some dykes in front of the German front-line trenches. On the left of the Garhwal Brigade, the Bareilly Brigade reached the German support trenches. By midday, however, their advanced position became precarious, as both flanks were exposed. They were forced to withdraw, owing to the enemy's counter-attacks.

Farther north, the 8th Division, of the III Corps, attacked two hours before zero from the vicinity of Bois Grenier, with the object of pushing through Fournes, and then joining up with the Indian Corps, who were to gain a footing on Aubers Ridge.

The assault was begun by three battalions, each on a 400-yard front, including Corner and Bridoux Forts. They were to be covered by smoke. Our assaulting battalions gained their objectives in the first rush, and one battalion reached the support trench.

Before nightfall, it was found necessary to withdraw back to our original trenches, which had, however, been improved in the course of the day.

Ten minutes earlier than the attack carried out by the III Corps, the 14th and 3rd Divisions, of the V Corps, farther north made an attack against the German positions on the Bellewaarde Ridge.

Two mines were exploded under the German trenches, and then five battalions of the 3rd Division and three battalions of the 14th Division, north of the 3rd Division, attacked.

South of the Ypres-Menin Road, these battalions of the 3rd Division were successful in capturing the German first-line trenches. The three battalions of the 14th Division were able to get into the German front-line trenches at different places on the Bellewaarde Ridge. Owing, however, to heavy artillery bombardment, followed by local German counter-attacks, our troops had to withdraw to their original trenches. South of the 2nd Division, who attacked in the vicinity of the La Bassée Canal, the 9th Division attacked with two brigades each on a front of 750 yards, towards the German trenches between Cité St. Élie and Haisnes. Their 3rd Brigade was then to carry forward the attack past Douvrin, a mile east of Haisnes, in order to join up with the 7th Division on their southern flank on the Haute Deule Canal, assisted in their final advance by the general reserve divisions of the XI Corps.

At zero hour, one battalion of the 26th Brigade started the assault, and within an hour had advanced 1,300 yards to the east of the Dump and Fosse 8. The other attacking battalion on the front of the 26th Brigade started to attack ten minutes after zero hour, and gained a position in line with, and on the north of, the first attacking battalion only five minutes later, in spite of their heavy casualties from the enemy's machine guns in Madagascar Point.

The 28th Brigade was unable to capture this important point, and so the whole of the 26th Brigade was unable to advance, owing to this lack of support on their left flank. The 28th Brigade had been able to sap forward a communication trench to connect our original line with the centre of the German Little Willie Trench, where half a company was maintaining its position.

Five companies of the 26th Brigade were able to get into the German last line of defence 1 hour and 35 minutes after zero hour.

Three and a half hours after zero, the reserve brigade of the 9th Division was ordered to attack Haisnes with three battalions, and to leave one battalion south-west of the Dump.

The commander of this brigade, however, had alternative orders, and decided to advance in the first instance to Pekin Trench to support our advanced company of the 26th Brigade, 2,000 yards east of our front line.

Two hours after the 9th Divisional Commander had given these orders, the troops of the 26th and 27th Brigades in Pekin Trench were in a dangerous position on a front of 1,200 yards, with both flanks exposed, as the German batteries had got the range of this trench, and their bombers, who were well supplied with grenades, were able to work up communication trenches to attack both flanks.

Gradually our troops were forced out of Pekin Trench, and the survivors withdrew back to Fosse Alley, where the 27th

1915 CAMPAIGN IN FRANCE

Brigade, with part of the 26th, was in touch with the 7th Division on the south, and continued to hold the line of this trench to the east of the Dump, where junction was made with the rest of the 26th Brigade, who carried the line round the Corons south-east of Madagascar Point. The bulk of the reserve brigade was back at the starting place. The 7th Division was south of the 9th Division. Their attack was made towards the northern part of Hulluch and Cité St. Elie on a front between the Vermelles-Hulluch Road to and excluding the Hohenzollern Redoubt.

It was carried out with two brigades, each with two forward and two reserve battalions. In two hours and a quarter after zero hour, one battalion of the 20th Brigade had gained a position east of the cross-roads on the Haisnes-La Bassée Road, 2,000 yards from their starting line. One battalion occupied trenches just west of Cité St. Elie.

The 22nd Brigade attacked on a two-battalion front of 800 yards.

One hour after zero, the German support trench on this front had been entered. The Brigade reserve advanced past the Quarries during the next hour, and reached Cité Trench. This advanced position could not be held, owing to heavy rifle and machine-gun fire. A position, however, was consolidated on the northern and eastern sides of the Quarries.

The 21st Brigade Commander, three hours after zero, sent two battalions to support the 20th Brigade and to advance on Hulluch, and also two battalions to support the 22nd Brigade and to capture St. Elie.

The battalions in their advance on Hulluch reached Gun Trench, 1,000 yards west of the village; the other two battalions reached a line beyond the southern edge of the Quarries.

Later, the ground gained was consolidated on the eastern and northern fronts of the Quarries, along Stone Alley, up to and including the southern end of the Quarries, then along Gun Trench from the Vermelles-Hulluch Road to Stone Alley. The further advance of the I Corps had not been possible, as there were no available reinforcements at hand to exploit success.

Three hours after zero, the general reserves—the 21st and 24th Divisions—had been placed at the disposal of the First Army Commander.

Two hours later, the heads of these two divisions were within three miles of our original first-line trenches. The Guards Division had been directed on Noeux-les-Mines, which they did not reach till 1800 hours, and the 28th Division was brought south of the River Lys from Bailleul.

Had these reserves been closer to the battlefield, there might have been excellent results, as two of the IV Corps' divisions had almost by mid-day reached the vicinity of Lens.

At zero hour, the IV Corps advanced against the German positions from Hulluch through Loos to the Double Crassier. The order of the divisions of this Corps from north to south was the 1st, 15th and 47th Divisions.

Two brigades of the 1st Division, with a third brigade in reserve, advanced on Hulluch and the heights south of it. The 1st Brigade on the north captured some gun positions, and reached the most western outskirts of Hulluch, west of the La Bassée-Haisnes Road, 400 yards west of the main part of the village.

The 2nd Brigade on the right of the 1st Brigade in the vicinity of Lone Tree was checked by barbed-wire entanglements which had not been destroyed. This caused a delay in our advance, and enabled the Germans to bring up their reserves to their rear trenches.

The 1st Brigade, however, was able, between 1400 hours and 1500 hours, to get in rear of the entanglement in front of our 2nd Brigade, and to capture some 500 Germans.

Two brigades of the 15th Division south of the 1st Division attacked on a two-brigade front. The 46th Brigade advanced to the north of Loos towards Hill 70; after capturing Loos Road Redoubt, the 44th Brigade on the south of the 46th Brigade advanced towards Loos and then to Hill 70. The 45th Brigade was in Divisional reserve.

Within one and a half hours after zero, the 44th Brigade was assaulting Loos from the north, while the 46th Brigade was attacking Chalk Pit Wood and Puits 14 bis. Four hours after zero, both brigades had seized Hill 70 and its redoubt.

On the southern flank of the First Army, the 141st and 140th Brigades attacked on a 1,200-yard front, from Double Crassier to Cemetery, 1,300 yards from the northern flank of the 141st Brigade on the left of the 47th Division. The 140th Brigade was south of the 141st, and two battalions of the 142nd Brigade continued our front for 1,200 yards due south to the Franco-British boundary.

Two companies of the 142nd Brigade were in Brigade reserve. At zero hour, the 140th and 141st Brigades advanced and drove the enemy from the greater part of the slag-heaps known as the Double Crassier.

The Bethune-Lens Road was then crossed, and the advance was continued to the Cemetery and the town of Loos. Farther south, however, the French Tenth Army, between Grenay and the Labyrinth, did not advance till 1225 hours, and then, as their direction was not towards Lens, but towards

1915 CAMPAIGN IN FRANCE

Souchez, the 47th Division, deployed between Grenay and Loos, had to form a defensive flank, and could not directly assist the 15th Division on Hill 70.

Twenty minutes after their zero hour, the French were on the eastern slopes of the Notre Dame de Lorette Plateau close to Hache Wood. Then the Souchez stream, half a mile farther west, was reached, but, owing to the strength of the enemy's defences, Generals Foch and d'Urbal decided to postpone their attack on Souchez till the following day.

In view of the small measure of success gained by our 1st Division, owing to the dangerous position of the 7th Division in the triangle St. Elie-Haisnes-Hulluch Quarries, of the 26th Brigade near Fosse 8, and owing to the check to the advance of the 28th Brigade on the Hohenzollern Redoubt, and the inability of the left wing of the I Corps to advance between this redoubt and the Bethune-La Bassée Canal, the Crown Prince of Bavaria on our front had an opportunity to deliver a counter-attack.

1030 hours: The 3rd Cavalry Division was ordered by the First Army Commander to march to Corons de Rutoire, with the object of capturing the high ground near Pont à Vendin when Cité St. Auguste had been taken.

1300 hours: The Germans were again in possession of Hill 70 Redoubt after their counter-attack made from Cité St. Laurent. Our 44th and 46th Brigades continued to hold a position from Loos Crassier along a line below Hill 70 Redoubt to Chalk Pit Wood.

1435 hours: The XI Corps Commander, who had previously been told that his 21st Division was to support the IV Corps, and his 24th Division was to support the I Corps after assembling on the line Mazingarbe-Vermelles, was now ordered to secure the passages of the Haute Deule Canal between Haisnes and Pont à Vendin.

The Guards Division was ordered to remain in general reserve.

1500 hours: The head of the 24th Division arrived at the Courant de Bally, two and a half miles from our original front-line trench.

2000 hours: The 47th and 15th Divisions were between the German first and second defensive lines from Double Crassier to Chalk Pit Wood. The 47th Division had formed a defensive flank facing in a south-easterly direction. Farther north, the 1st and 7th Divisions had reached the Lens-La Bassée Road west of Hulluch.

The 9th Division was in possession of the Dump, Fosse 8, and Hohenzollern Redoubt. Our northern division had,

G

owing to very difficult conditions on their front, been obliged to reoccupy their original trenches.

Our casualties up to this time were nearly a sixth of the forces engaged.

The XI Corps was ordered to advance to the Hulluch-Lens Road. These orders were later cancelled, and the 21st and 24th Divisions were on the move in the Loos Valley, for the greater part of the night.

The 21st Division reached a position north of the 15th Division near Chalk Pit Wood; the 24th Division reached a position south of the 1st Division east of the Loos-Haisnes Road along Alley 4.

September 26th.—0100 hours: the Germans counter-attacked, our troops holding the Quarries and Fosse 8. The 20th Brigade withdrew to Gun Trench, which now became our front line. The Germans also attacked our 21st Brigade in the Quarries from the gap between this brigade and the 27th Brigade farther north.

0130 hours: The Germans occupied the Quarries. Quarry Trench was occupied as our forward position. The 21st, 27th, and 22nd Brigades were now in contact with each other.

0645 hours: A battalion of the 71st Brigade made a counter-attack against the Germans in the Quarries. This was checked by heavy rifle and machine-gun fire.

The 26th Brigade repulsed a German attack on Fosse 8. The 73rd Brigade relieved the 26th Brigade.

0900 hours: The Commander of the First Army directed that there was to be a general assault on the whole Army front between and including Hill 70 and Cité St. Elie. These objectives were to be captured by the 15th Division and 62nd Brigade attached to it, and by the I Corps.

The I Corps was to be responsible for the capture of Hulluch and Cité St. Elie, the 15th Division and 62nd Brigade were to capture Hill 70. The 21st and 24th Divisions were to pass through the German second positions between Bois Hugo and Hulluch.

Three battalions of the 45th Brigade started their attack to the redoubt on Hill 70. They were supported by two battalions of the 62nd Brigade. A position was gained through the centre of the redoubt.

1000 hours: German infantry from their 26th Regiment made a counter-attack against the open left flank of the 63rd Brigade. This attack was checked.

1030 hours: A German counter-attack started against our positions running south-west from Chalk Pit Wood. Troops in these positions, as well as the troops of the 63rd and 64th

1915 CAMPAIGN IN FRANCE

Brigades who were advancing to attack, fell back across the Lens-La Bassée Road. The troops in Chalk Pit Wood held their positions.

1100 hours: The Germans started a heavy bombardment on our forward position at Hill 70. The 45th and 46th Brigades occupied positions on the west side of Hill 70 below the top of the hill. Two battalions of the 72nd Brigade and the 2nd Welch Regiment began to advance from their trenches 200 yards west of the Loos-Haisnes Road into the Loos Valley. These battalions were supported by two battalions of the 71st Brigade.

The attacking battalions came under heavy fire west of the Lens-La Bassée Road.

1200 hours: The 6th Cavalry Brigade, less one regiment, started on foot to occupy the old German first-line trench, 1,000 yards west of Loos on a front of 600 yards. The attack of the leading battalions of the 1st Division west of Hulluch was brought to a standstill.

Part of the 62nd Brigade was still holding a line through the western side of Hill 70 from Loos Crassier to Chalet Wood. The Germans held Bois Hugo and Puits 13 bis.

1220 hours: Our battalions of the 63rd and 64th Brigades advancing east of the Lens-La Bassée Road came under heavy fire from Chalet Wood and Bois Hugo, and they were forced to retreat to the Grenay-Hulluch Road.

1300 hours: Between Bois Hugo and Puits 13 bis, parties of men from the 72nd Brigade reached a position close to the German second line. Some men of the 2nd Welch Regiment got into a German trench south of Hulluch. This was the limit of the advance of the 21st Division.

1330 hours: General retirement began to Lone Tree Ridge. There was a general retirement from Hill 70 through Loos village. Troops of the 2nd Division advanced to a position 200 yards west of the Quarries on their left, and on the right in touch with the 7th Division. They were on a front of 600 yards in their new positions.

1600 hours: Orders were issued for the XI Corps to hold the original German first line of trenches. The Guards Division was placed at the disposal of the First Army Commander.

1700 hours: The withdrawal of the XI Corps ended.

1800 hours: The 2nd Guards Brigade reached Corons de Rutoire. The 1st Guards Brigade reached Vermelles.

2000 hours: The 3rd Dragoon Guards reoccupied the Crassier. Parties of the 15th Division reoccupied a line of trenches on the western side of Hill 70 with the dismounted Royal Dragoons.

H

2330 hours: The remainder of the dismounted 3rd Cavalry Division started to reoccupy Loos.

September 27th.—0400 hours: The 1st and 2nd Guards Brigades relieved troops in the trenches north of Loos between those held by the 6th Cavalry Brigade and the 1st Division in Gun Trench. This relief stabilized the situation south of the Vermelles-Hulluch Road.

0500 hours: The Germans bombarded intensively our trenches near the Dump and the Hohenzollern Redoubt, and attacked the 21st Brigade in Stone Alley.

1200 hours: Our troops, having been forced to withdraw from the vicinity of the Hohenzollern Redoubt and the Dump, occupied a new line of trenches east of the redoubt.

1400 hours: Two Corps of the French Tenth Army started an attack. This was stopped an hour later, owing to strong hostile opposition.

1500 hours: The 26th Brigade was ordered to retake the Dump and Fosse trenches. This brigade was able to reach the eastern face of the Hohenzollern Redoubt, when the Germans counter-attacked from both sides of the Dump, and we were forced to withdraw in this area from Fosse Alley and the Redoubt back to the German original front line.

1600 hours: The Guards Division began to advance from their front-line trenches. Their objectives were Hill 70, Puits 14 bis, and Chalk Pit Wood.

1700 hours: Parties of the 2nd Guards Brigade reached Chalk Pit Wood and Puits buildings, and a general line was occupied from the southern end of Chalk Pit Wood towards Loos. The Puits being effectively commanded by well-posted machine guns, it was not possible to maintain a position there.

1800 hours: The Welsh Guards, of the 3rd Guards Brigade, attacked the German trenches on Hill 70, and were able to reach a position about 100 yards from the redoubt on this hill. The 47th Division started to attack Chalk Pit Copse.

1930 hours: The 47th Division captured their objective and a strong point near it on the Lens-Bethune Road, and repulsed a strong counter-attack.

2300 hours: The 3rd Guards Brigade consolidated the position gained below the crest of Hill 70 to connect with the 3rd Cavalry Division on their right and back to the Loos-Hulluch Road on their left.

September 28th.—The Commander-in-Chief discussed plans with the French Tenth Army Commander, who agreed to send a Corps to take over the ground from the French left up to and including Hill 70 and the village of Loos, as it was not considered that the advance of the French Tenth Army afforded adequate protection to our flank.

Our line now required more men to hold it than formerly, as there were many salients in it which added to the length of the trench to be held, and as we had captured a double line of trench 6,500 yards long.

For the work done on this day, the Despatches give the following concise account:—

"The 28th was passed in consolidating the ground gained and in making a certain number of internal moves of divisions in order to give the troops rest and to enable those units whose casualties had been heavy to refill their ranks with reinforcements. The 47th Division made a little more ground on the south, capturing one field gun and a few machine guns; on the evening of this day the situation remained practically unchanged."

September 29th.—It was agreed with the French Commander to begin further operations on October 2nd. The Germans were able to gain some ground near the Hohenzollern Redoubt after suffering heavy casualties. The advance of the 1st Coldstream Guards from Chalk Pit Wood was ineffective, owing to heavy machine-gun fire by the Germans from Bois Hugo.

September 30th.—Consolidation was carried out on the whole front. A new trench line was started between Chalk Pit Wood and Alley 4. The Germans captured 250 yards of our Gun Trenches on the front held by the 7th Division.

General Foch visited the Commander-in-Chief and informed him that the plan for the next offensive would be a simultaneous attack by their Tenth and our First Armies, to eliminate the German salient. The First Army would attack in a south-easterly direction on a three-mile front; the Tenth Army would attack towards Mericourt and Avion in a north-easterly direction on a similar front.

October 2nd.—Owing to the difficulties of carrying out internal moves, in view of the fact that German observers overlooked our positions from Hill 70 and from the Dump, the general offensive was postponed until October 6th.

October 3rd.—Two regiments and a battalion from the German XIX Corps recaptured the whole of the Hohenzollern Redoubt.

October 6th.—The French Armies renewed their attacks in Champagne.

October 8th.—1200 hours: The German bombardment of our whole front began.

1600 hours: About ten battalions of the German 7th and 8th Divisions attacked the French IX Corps, while their 153rd and 216th Regiments attacked our 1st Division from south-west of Puits 14 bis to the north of the Chalk Pit. Other attacks were made against our troops in Quarry Trench and Big Willie by approximately six battalions of the German 117th and 14th Divisions.

1800 hours: The 37th Brigade made an unsuccessful attempt to regain 250 yards of Gun Trench north of the Vermelles-Hulluch Road.

The German attacks were finally repulsed after heavy losses from our machine-gun and artillery fire.

October 11th.—The French offensive operations gained little results, either on Hill 70 or towards the crest of Vimy Ridge. The 2nd Grenadier Guards captured and held a length of trench south of the Dump.

October 12th.—The Germans made a bombing attack in an unsuccessful attempt to recapture the trenches gained by the Grenadier Guards.

October 13th.—1200 hours: The First Army began a two hours' bombardment of the German positions with 540 guns and howitzers.

1300 hours: Gas was discharged from our front for fifty minutes, and smoke screens were started.

1400 hours: Our attacks began with five battalions of the 1st Brigade advancing against the German positions on the Lens-La Bassée Road on a front of 1,400 yards west and south-west of Hulluch.

The 1st Brigade advanced up to the enemy's wire entanglements, but was unable to get through the four gaps that had been cut by artillery fire.

After dark, the survivors of this brigade withdrew to their own trenches.

Two brigades of the 12th Division made an attack on the Quarries.

The 37th Brigade gained the southern part of Stone Alley, and the 35th Brigade captured part of the south-western edge of the Quarries.

The 46th Brigade made an attempt to capture the Hohenzollern Redoubt, Fosse 8, and the Dump. The 137th Brigade was to advance across the Big Willie Trench and to occupy Fosse Alley beyond it. The 138th Brigade was to advance to the Corons north of the Dump. They were able to gain a footing in Fosse Trench and the buildings of the Corons. They were unable to advance beyond the Hohenzollern Redoubt.

The 2nd Division north of this redoubt was unable to make progress.

1445 hours: Reinforcements of two companies reached the northern end of Hohenzollern Redoubt.

October 14th.—0400 hours: A German counter-attack towards our new line constructed on the western side of the Hohenzollern Redoubt was defeated. The French IX Corps remained on the western slope of Hill 70. Our First Army retained their positions from the La Bassée Canal south to the Vermelles-Auchy Road, along the western side of the Hohenzollern Redoubt and the trenches west of the Lens-La Bassée Road along the eastern and southern sides of Chalk Pit Wood to a point 500 yards west of the Lens-La Bassée Road and the northern edge of Chalet Wood.

" Notwithstanding the stalemate and the heavy losses, the battle of Loos was far from shaking the faith of the officers and men of the B.E.F. in their power to break through the German line; indeed, their confidence was only increased thereby. Many had seen, all knew, that the line had been broken, for they had the satisfaction of seeing prisoners and captured material. There were the definite results that 8,000 yards of German front had been taken, including localities fortified at leisure by all the experience and skill of the German engineers. In places the British troops had advanced over two miles from their front line, the largest advance made by the Allies on the western front since trench warfare had begun. That more had not been accomplished at Loos was attributed by the troops to bad luck and a succession of accidents. Finally, all ranks had gained experience, and for the first time it became possible to draw up reasoned instructions, founded on the battle, as to the methods to be pursued if an assault was to be a success under the new conditions."[*]

There was now a time of comparative quiet on our part of the front.

During this Battle of Loos, we captured approximately 3,000 prisoners, 26 guns and 40 machine guns; we advanced our line about 3,200 yards on a front of 8,000 yards, and we had gained valuable experience on which to make plans for the future. The main lesson was to train men and to build up large stores of ammunition with which to support

[*] Official History of the War; Vol. IV: Military Operations, France and Belgium, 1915.

either our advances or the attempts of the enemy to recapture our positions.

Although during this year of 1915, our operations in the Dardanelles failed, and in Mesopotamia were at a standstill at Kut, though Serbia and Montenegro had been overrun by the Germans, who were across the frontier of Russia, yet we had begun to realize the value of concentration of force and of resources, which, as our Regulations tell us, is essential for the achievement of success.

APPENDIX

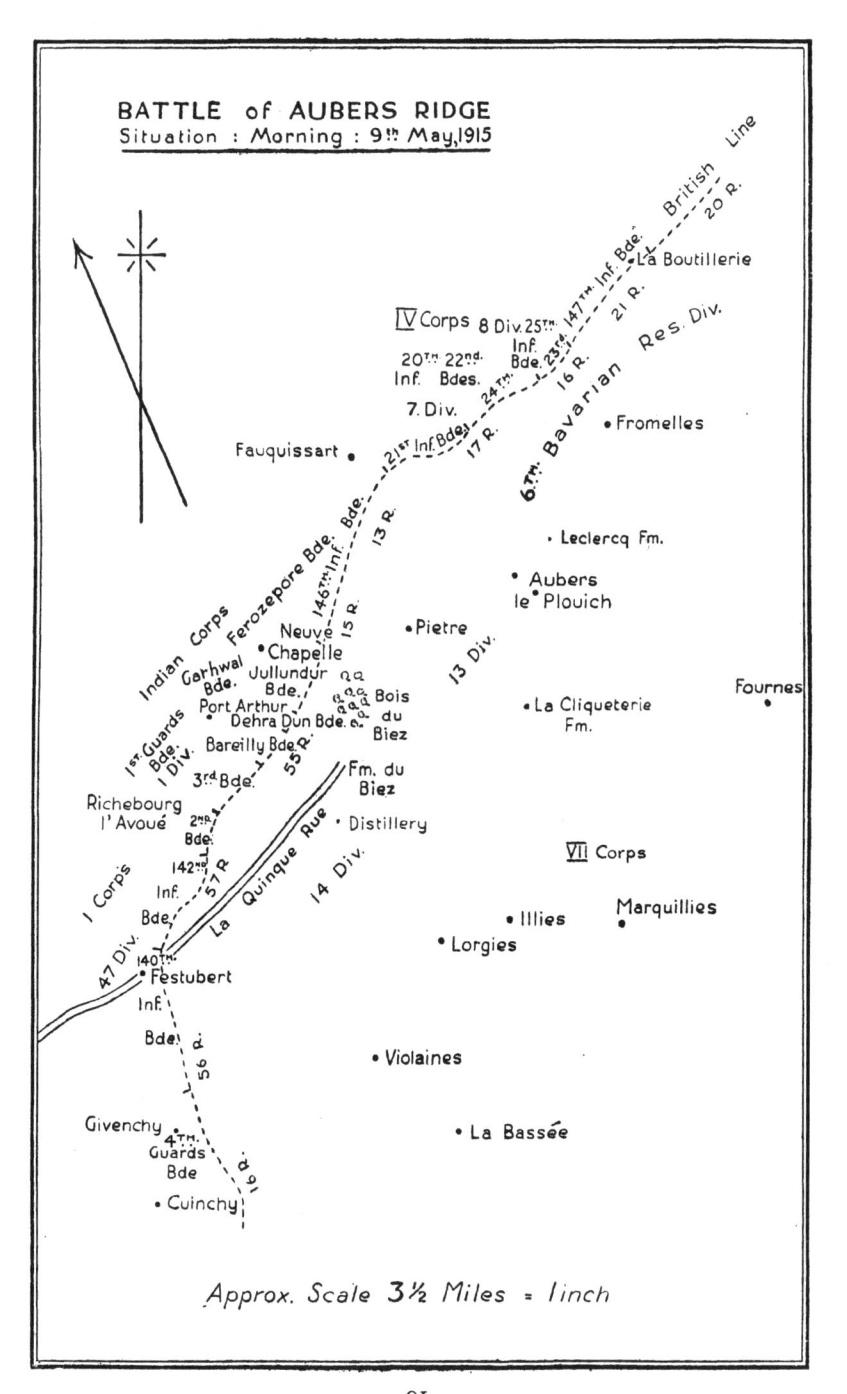

BATTLE of AUBERS RIDGE
Situation : Morning : 9th May, 1915

BATTLE of FESTUBERT : May 15TH – 25TH

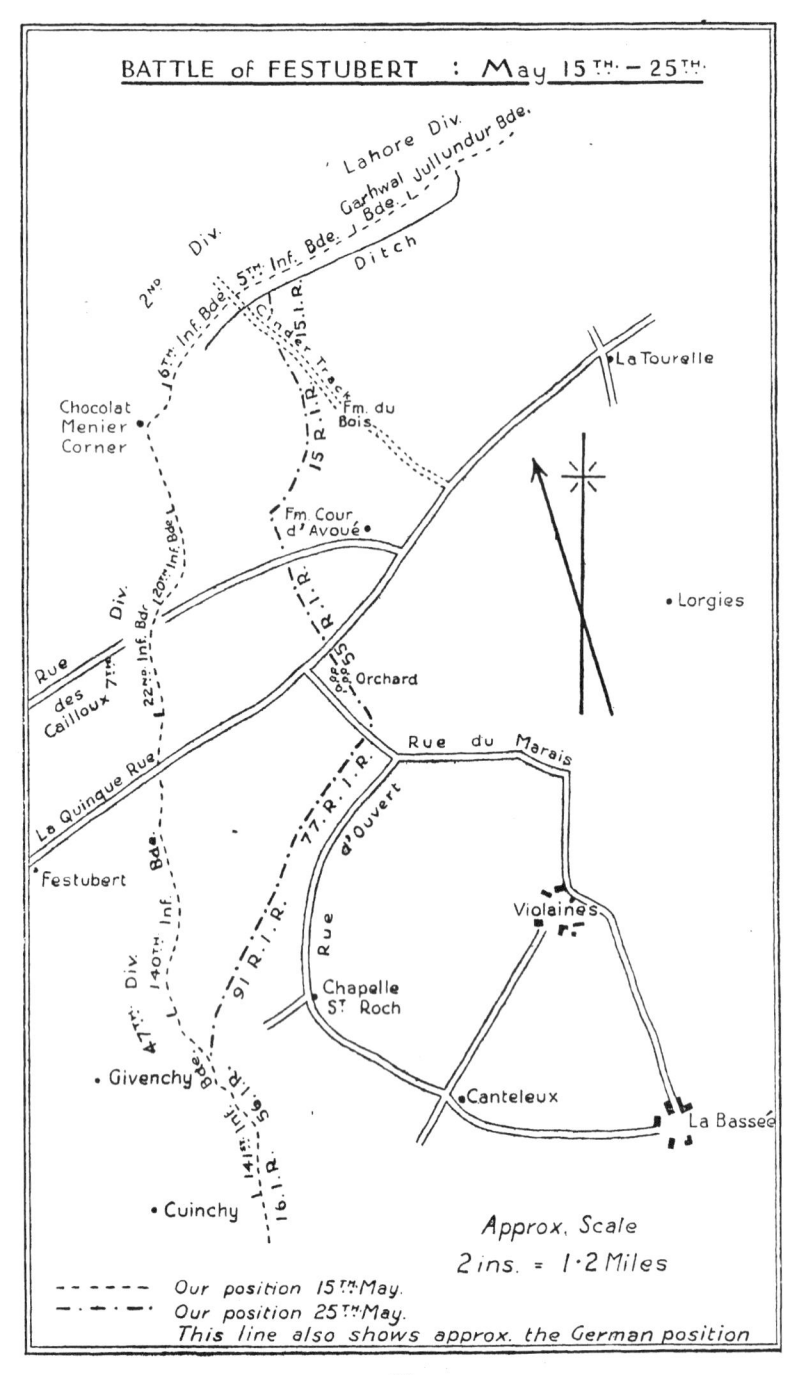

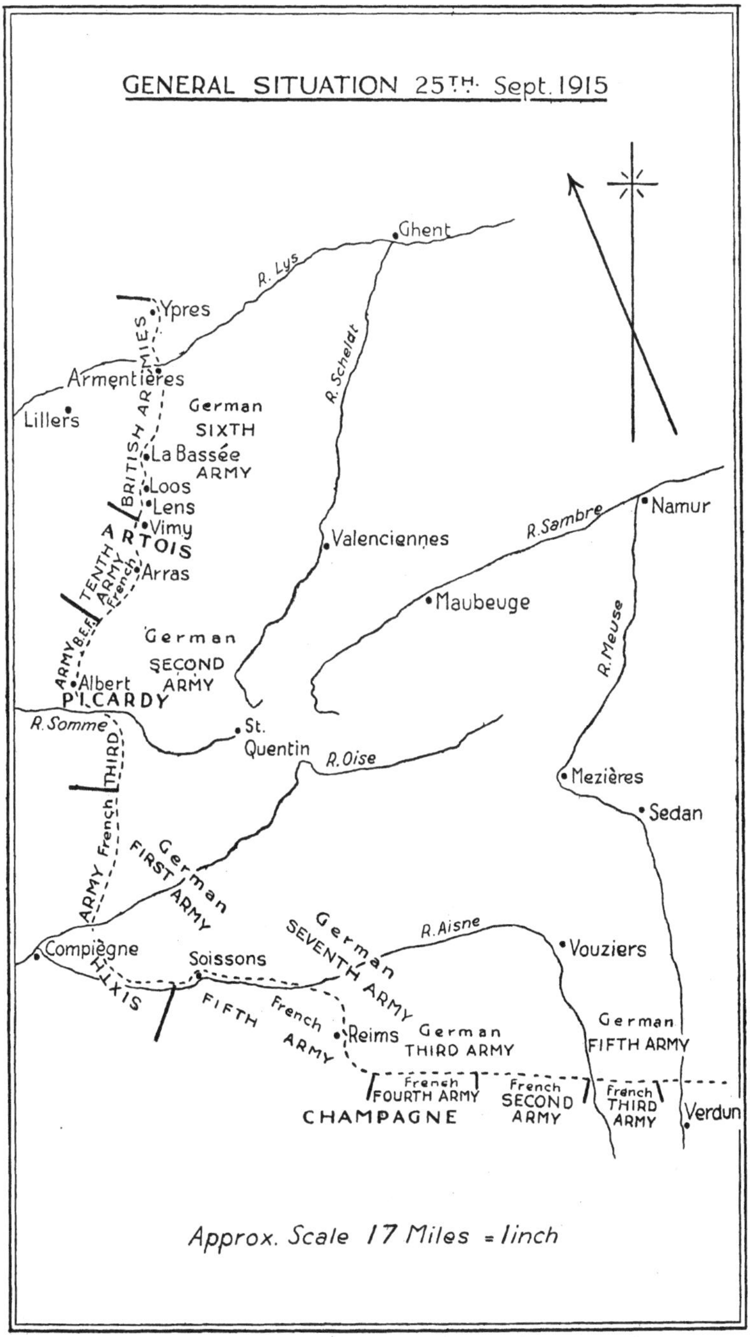
GENERAL SITUATION 25TH. Sept. 1915
Ghent
R. Lys
Ypres
Armentières
Lillers
BRITISH ARMIES
German
SIXTH
ARMY
La Bassée
Loos
Lens
Vimy
ARTOIS
Arras
TENTH ARMY French
ARMY B.E.F.
R. Scheldt
Valenciennes
R. Sambre
Namur
Maubeuge
R. Meuse
German
SECOND
ARMY
Albert
PICARDY
R. Somme
St. Quentin
R. Oise
THIRD
French
ARMY
Mezières
Sedan
German
FIRST
ARMY
Compiègne
Soissons
SIXTH
FIFTH
French
ARMY
German
SEVENTH ARMY
R. Aisne
Vouziers
Reims
German
THIRD ARMY
German
FIFTH ARMY
French
FOURTH ARMY
French
SECOND
ARMY
French
THIRD
ARMY
Verdun
CHAMPAGNE
Approx. Scale 17 Miles = 1 inch

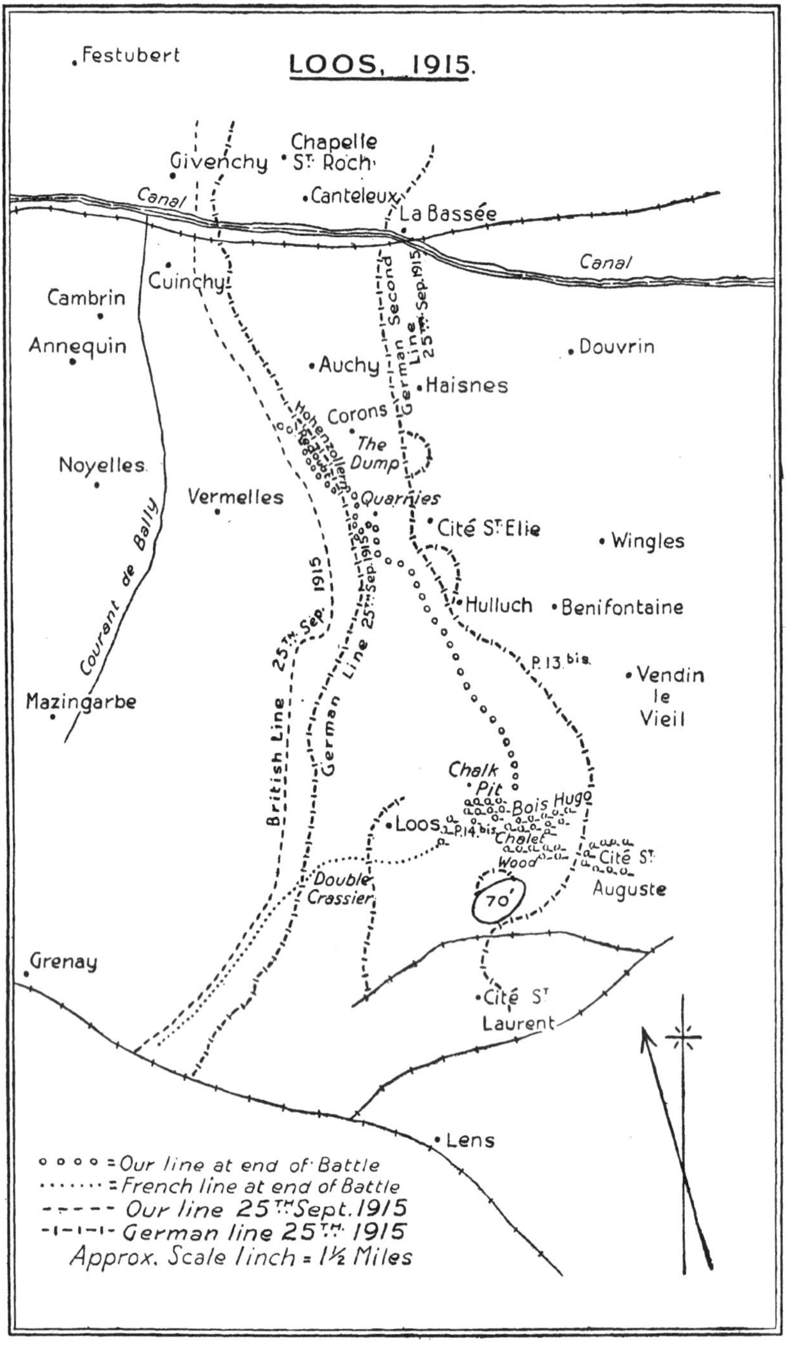
LOOS, 1915.
Festubert
Chapelle St. Roch
Givenchy
Canteleux
Canal
La Bassée
Canal
Cuinchy
Cambrin
Annequin
Second German Line 25th Sep. 1915
Douvrin
Auchy
Haisnes
Hohenzollern Redoubt
Corons
The Dump
Noyelles
Vermelles
Quarries
Cité St. Elie
Wingles
Courant de Bally
British Line 25th Sep. 1915
German Line 25th Sep. 1915
Hulluch
Benifontaine
P. 13 bis.
Vendin le Vieil
Mazingarbe
Chalk Pit
Bois Hugo
Loos
P. 14 bis.
Chalet Wood
Cité St. Auguste
Double Crassier
70
Grenay
Cité St. Laurent
Lens
o o o o = Our line at end of Battle
.... = French line at end of Battle
- - - - Our line 25th Sept. 1915
-·-·-· German line 25th 1915
Approx. Scale 1 inch = 1½ Miles

INDEX

A

Ablain St. Nazaire, 5, 17.
Adalbert Alley, 69.
Adriatic, 6.
Africa, South-West, 3, 72.
Africa, 21.
Aisne, River, 93.
Aix-Noulette, 19.
Albert, 14.
Allennes, 15, 43.
Alley, No. 1, 19.
Alley, No. 4, 41, 82, 85.
Alley, A., 47.
Alliance, German, 3.
Allies, 3, 4, 7, 22.
Alsace, 3.
Angres, 17, 18, 43.
Annequin, 94.
Ardennes, 6.
Armentières, 26, 93.
Army, British :
   First, 4, 7, 15, 18, 19, 23, 24, 28, 31, 38, 43, 45, 46, 47, 49, 60, 63, 64, 66, 69, 72, 73, 74, 79, 80, 83, 85, 93.
   Second, 9, 21, 23, 58, 63, 93.
   Third, 93.
Army, French :
   Second, 21, 93.
   Third, 21, 93.
   Fourth, 21, 93.
   Fifth, 21, 57, 93.
   Sixth, 93.
   Tenth, 4, 6, 7, 8, 9, 12, 14, 15, 16, 17, 21, 23, 25, 42, 43, 45, 50, 55, 57, 58, 60, 63, 66, 68, 72, 80, 84, 85, 93.
Army, German :
   First, 93
   Second, 14, 15, 93.
   Third, 63, 72, 93.
   Fourth, 63.
   Fifth, 93.
   Sixth, 8, 9, 14, 43, 66, 72, 93.
   Seventh, 14, 15.
Arras, 4, 14, 17, 19, 21, 23, 63, 72, 93.
Artois, 3, 14, 15, 22, 23, 57, 63, 72, 73
Ath, 21, 23.
Auberive, 6.

Aubers Ridge, 1, 4, 6, 7, 8, 15, 20, 23, 27, 30, 32, 63, 64, 66, 75, 77, 91.
Auchy, 18, 24, 25, 40, 41, 43, 44, 48, 62, 87, 94.
Auchy Alley, 18.
Auchel-aux-Bois, 15, 20, 43.
Australia, 6.
Austrians, 7, 22, 25, 71.
Avion, 60, 85.

B

Bailleul, 4, 8, 67, 79.
Balkans, 3.
Barter's Force, 67, 69.
Bauvin, 6, 8, 21, 23, 64.
Bavarian Regiment, First, 4, 8.
Bavarian 15th Division, 47.
Bavarian Crown Prince, 46.
Beau Puits, 9, 11, 12, 13, 67.
Belgium, 49.
Bellewaarde, 77, 78.
Benifontaine, 94.
Béthune, 15, 17, 19, 20, 45, 46, 47, 55, 80, 84.
Beuvry, 15, 43.
Big Willie Trench, 18, 60, 8f
Bixschoote, 63.
Blankenberghe, 23.
Boesinghe, 14, 72.
Bois Carre, 52.
Bois de Berthonvale, 5.
Bois des Dames, 43.
Bois du Biez, 91.
Bois-en-Hache, 17, 18.
Bois Grenier, 77.
Bois Hugo, 16, 24, 25, 51, 53, 56, 58, 82, 85, 94.
Botha, General, 3, 72.
Brigade :
   Guards, 36, 37, 67, 68, 70, 71, 83, 84, 91.
   1st, 29, 47, 63, 65, 80, 86.
   2nd, 27, 29, 47, 65.
   2nd Canadian, 70.
   3rd, 27, 29, 30, 65, 78, 91.
   3rd Canadian, 37, 70. 71,
   5th, 24, 32, 33, 68, 69, 76, 77, 92.
   6th, 32, 33, 36, 69, 70, 76, 92.
   6th Cavalry, 83, 84.
   19th, 76.
   20th, 35, 36, 68, 69, 79, 92.

INDEX

Brigade (contd.):
21st, 36, 37, 65, 68, 70, 71, 79, 82, 84, 91.
22nd, 34, 35, 36, 68, 69, 79, 82, 92.
23rd, 65, 91.
24th, 31, 65, 91.
25th, 31, 65, 66, 91.
26th, 25, 48, 78, 79, 81, 82.
27th, 25, 48, 78, 82.
28th, 78, 81.
35th, 86.
37th, 86.
44th, 47, 80, 83.
45th, 80, 82, 83.
46th, 47, 80, 86.
58th, 77.
63rd, 82, 83.
64th, 82, 83.
71st, 82, 83.
73rd, 83.
137th, 86.
140th, 80, 91, 92.
141st, 92.
142nd, 71, 91.
147th, 91
Bareilly, 29, 77, 91.
Dehra Dun, 27, 28, 91.
Ferozepore, 91.
Garhwal, 32, 33, 67, 68, 77, 91, 92.
Jullundur, 33, 66, 91, 92.
German Guards' Reserve, 71.
Bulgaria, 3, 72.

C

Calonne, 68.
Cambrai, 6, 19.
Cambrin, 94.
Cameroons, 3, 71.
Canal La Bassée, 19, 20, 24, 25, 40, 43, 44, 58, 59, 66, 67, 72, 73, 76, 77, 78, 81, 87, 94.
Canteleux, 20, 24, 73, 92, 94.
Carency, 5, 17.
Carvin, 19, 21, 23, 24.
Cassel, 67.
Casualties, 2, 5, 13, 25.
Chalet Wood, 25, 47, 53, 83, 87.
Chalk Pit, 43, 45, 55, 56, 62, 86, 93.
Chalk Pit Wood, 16, 47, 55, 56, 57, 62, 80, 81, 82, 83, 84, 85, 87.
Champagne, 6, 14, 15, 22, 23, 48, 57, 72, 73, 93.
Chapelle St. Roch, 11, 12, 13, 38, 67, 70, 73, 92, 94.
Chocolat Menier Corner, 11, 92.
Cinder Track, 70.
Cité St. Auguste, 16, 18, 24, 41, 43, 46, 48, 51, 75, 76, 81, 94.

Cité St. Edouard, 16.
Cité St. Elie, 16, 18, 19, 24, 26, 40, 41, 42, 43, 46, 47, 48, 50, 52, 62, 75, 76, 78, 79, 94.
Cité St. Laurent, 25, 57, 76, 81, 94.
Cité Trench, 79.
Coldstream Guards, 85.
Commander-in-Chief, 5, 26, 47, 58, 63, 66, 67, 70, 84.
Compiègne, 93.
Condé, 21, 23, 72.
Constantinople, 14.
Corner, 77.
Corons Alley, 18.
Corons, 47, 79, 86, 94.
Corps, British:
I, 4, 6, 8, 9, 15, 20, 24, 26, 30, 36, 37, 42, 43, 44, 57, 64, 70, 71, 73, 79, 81, 82, 91.
III, 20, 21, 43, 58, 72, 77.
IV, 4, 6, 8, 15, 20, 24, 26, 30, 42, 43, 44, 46, 64, 65, 66, 73, 80, 91.
V, 59, 77.
XI, 20, 25, 26, 44, 51, 52, 53, 58, 72, 78, 81, 83.
Cavalry, 21-23, 72.
Indian, 4, 6, 8, 10, 20, 23, 24, 26, 29, 30, 36, 58, 64, 66, 70, 72, 76, 91.
Indian Cavalry, 8, 15, 23.
Corps, French:
IX, 4, 86, 87.
X, 4.
XVII, 4, 8.
XX, 4.
XXI, 4-8.
XXXIII, 4.
Corps, German:
VII, 4, 9, 13, 67.
XIV, 4.
XIX, 85.
Courrières, 20, 21, 23.
Cuinchy, 91, 92, 94.

D

Dardanelles, 6, 9, 12, 21, 72, 88.
Defence Committee, 1.
Deynze, 23.
Distillery, 91.
Divisions, British:
Guards, 15, 43, 55, 79, 81, 83.
1st, 4, 8, 13, 15, 24, 27, 43, 45, 64, 65, 67, 68, 71, 80, 82, 86, 91.
2nd, 4, 9, 10, 11, 13, 15, 24, 32, 36, 37, 64, 67, 68, 69, 70, 71, 73, 78, 87, 92.

INDEX

Divisions, British (*contd.*):
3rd, 77.
7th, 9, 10, 11, 13, 15, 24, 30, 33, 34, 36, 37, 43, 45, 64, 66, 67, 68, 69, 70, 71, 79, 91, 92.
8th, 14, 30, 66.
9th, 15, 24, 44, 55, 79, 81.
14th, 77.
15th, 15, 45, 46, 55, 74, 80, 81, 83.
21st, 15, 43, 47, 53, 54, 79, 82.
24th, 15, 43, 47, 54, 79, 81, 82.
27th, 63.
28th, 58, 63, 79.
47th, 9, 13, 15, 24, 37, 38, 45, 56, 64, 67, 68, 71, 80, 81, 84, 85, 91, 92.
49th, 4.
50th, 4, 64.
51st, 4, 9, 64, 71.
71st, 37.
Canadian, 4, 9, 37, 38, 64, 68.
Cavalry, 4, 15, 20, 43, 46, 55, 58, 64.
Lahore, 4, 9, 43, 68, 92.
Meerut, 4, 8, 9, 13, 43, 65, 66, 77.
Divisions, German:
7th, 86.
8th, 15, 43, 65, 91.
12th, 86.
13th, 91.
14th, 13, 43, 86, 91.
58th, 4, 8.
115th, 4, 8.
117th, 43.
Bavarian Reserve, 4, 91.
Guard Reserve, 15, 43.
Don, 6, 8, 23, 64.
Douai, 3, 4, 5, 6, 9, 15, 17, 21, 23, 72.
Double Crassier, 18, 24, 40, 41, 42, 43, 45, 47, 60, 80, 94.
Douvrin, 19, 78, 84.
Doullens, 72.
Dover Patrol, 23.
Dragoons, Royal, 83.
Dragoon Guards, 3rd, 83.
Dump, 18, 19, 24, 41, 44, 55, 59, 78, 81, 84, 85, 86, 94.
Dutch frontier, 23.

E

East Africa, 6, 14.
Ecurie, 8.
Egypt, 6, 14.
England, 9, 12.
Euphrates, 71.
Europe, 3.

F

Falkland Islands, Battle of, 6.
Farbus, 8, 17.
Fauquissart, 91.
Fecht, River, 3.
Ferme du Bois, 69, 70, 92.
Ferme Cour d'Avoué, 37, 68, 69, 70, 92.
Ferme du Biez, 91.
Festubert, 1, 9, 11, 13, 22, 23, 32, 66, 67, 68, 91, 92, 94.
Flying Corps, Royal, 4, 13, 22, 64, 67, 73.
Fleet, German, 6.
Fleet, Austrian, 6.
Foch, General, 9, 17, 81, 84.
Fosse Alley, 41, 48, 49, 78, 86.
Fosse 8, 16, 18, 19, 24, 40, 42, 44, 45, 46, 49, 55, 61, 81, 82, 86.
Fosse Trench, 18, 19, 61, 84, 86.
Fournes, 5, 8, 63, 77, 91
French, 3, 7, 9, 10, 12, 13, 15, 16, 23, 26, 46, 55, 59, 60, 72, 73, 85.
Fromelles, 6, 8, 63, 66, 91.
Front, Eastern, 4, 12.
Front, Western, 3, 4, 7, 10, 14, 21, 22, 25, 72.

G

Galicia, 3, 7.
Gallipoli, 14.
Gas, 2, 11, 13, 15, 19, 23, 57, 63, 86.
Germans, 2, 3, 4, 5, 6, 7, 8, 9, 10, 12, 14, 15, 16, 17, 18, 19, 20, 22, 25, 26, 27, 29, 30, 33, 35, 37, 42, 46, 47, 53, 59, 60, 65, 66, 68, 74, 77, 78, 82, 83, 86.
Germany, 2, 3.
Ghent, 93.
Givenchy, 6, 17, 20, 38, 91, 92, 94.
Gorlice, 4, 63.
Greece, 3.
Grenades, 2, 12, 13.
Grenadier Guards, 68, 86.
Grenay, 14, 16, 19, 24, 26, 41, 42, 44, 48, 53, 58, 72, 73, 94.
Gully Ravine, 71.
Gun Trench, 79, 82, 84.

H

Haisnes, 16, 17, 18, 19, 20, 24, 25, 26, 40, 41, 42, 43, 45, 47, 48, 73, 75, 78, 79, 80, 81, 83, 94.
Haute Deule Canal, 6, 8, 20, 21, 23, 24, 43, 50, 57, 64, 72, 73, 78, 81.

INDEX

Haut Pommereau, 5.
Henin-Liétard, 21, 23.
Hill 60, 73.
Hill 70, 16, 18, 24, 25, 40, 41, 43, 45, 46, 47, 50, 51, 52, 54, 55, 56, 57, 58, 59, 60, 75, 80, 81, 82, 83, 84, 85, 86, 94.
Hill 119, 17.
Hohenzollern Redoubt, 18, 20, 24, 40, 42, 43, 44, 47, 49, 55, 58, 59, 61, 62, 79, 81, 84, 85, 86, 87.
Hulluch, 16, 17, 18, 19, 20, 24, 25, 41, 42, 43, 45, 46, 47, 48, 50, 51, 52, 53, 54, 62, 75, 79, 80, 81, 82, 83, 84, 86, 94.

I

Illies, 91.
India, 6, 21.
Irish Rifles, Royal, 65.
Italians, 9, 72.
Italy, 7, 71.

J

Jäger Battalions, 15, 43, 69, 73.
Japanese, 3.
Joffre, Marshal, 15, 22, 63.

K

Knocke, 23.
Krithia, 9, 71.
Kut, 21, 88.

L

La Bassée, 5, 8, 15, 16, 17, 18, 19, 20, 23, 25, 26, 41, 42, 43, 44, 46, 48, 49, 52, 53, 54, 55, 56, 59, 60, 62, 63, 67, 72, 79, 80, 83, 86, 87, 91, 97.
La Boutillerie, 91.
Labyrinth, 10, 14, 17.
La Cliqueterie Farm, 6, 20, 66, 91.
La Folie, 17.
Langemarck, 63.
Laon, 6.
La Plouich, 91.
La Quinque Rue, 11, 13, 33, 36, 67, 69, 70, 91, 92.
La Targette, 17.
La Tourelle, 92.
Leclercq Farm, 91.
Le Nouvion, 73.
Lens, 5, 7, 9, 14, 15, 16, 17, 18, 19, 21, 23, 24, 25, 40, 41, 43, 45, 47, 48, 50, 53, 55, 59, 60, 80, 82, 83, 84, 86, 87, 93, 94.
Les Eparges, 3.

Liévin, 17, 18, 43.
Lille, 3, 5, 6, 13, 15, 17, 21, 23, 67, 72.
Lillers, 20, 72, 93.
Little Willie Trench, 18, 61, 78.
Loison, 60.
London Regiment, 1/13th, 65, 66.
Lone Tree, 45, 83.
Loos, 8, 14, 16, 17, 18, 19, 20, 21, 24, 25, 39, 41, 43, 44, 45, 46, 47, 48, 49, 50, 52, 53, 54, 56, 57, 58, 62, 72, 73, 74, 82, 83, 84, 87, 93, 94.
Loos Pylons, 16.
Loos Redoubt, 43, 44, 80.
Lords, House of, 10.
Lorgies, 36, 69, 91, 92.
Lys River, 5, 79, 93.

M

Machine Guns, 7, 10, 12, 28, 30, 33, 37, 38, 55, 84.
Mackensen, von, 6, 63.
Madagascar Point, 78, 79.
Madagascar Trench, 18.
Marne, River, 13.
Marquillies, 91.
Maubeuge, 93.
Mazingarbe, 81, 94.
Menin, 77.
Mericourt, 60, 85.
Mesopotamia, 21, 71, 88.
Meuse, River, 15, 72, 93.
Mezières, 6, 21, 93.
Middleskercke, 23.
Ministry of Munitions, 22.
Mons, 22.
Mont St. Eloi, 5.
Montenegro, 88.
Morale, 5, 10, 52.

N

Namur, 22, 93.
Nancy, 63.
Navy, British, 1.
Neuve Chapelle, 3, 5, 6, 7, 8, 12, 20, 49, 66, 72, 91.
Neuville St. Vaast, 10, 13, 14, 17.
New Zealand, 6.
Nœux-les-Mines, 15, 19, 43, 47, 53, 54, 55, 79.
Northamptonshire Regiment, 65.
North Breastwork, 69.
North Face, 61.
Notre Dame de Lorette, 5, 7, 8, 17, 18, 81.
Noyelles, 94.
Noyon, 14, 23.

INDEX

O
Official History, Vol IV, 7, 75.
Oise, River, 93.
Orchard, 68, 92.

P
Pacific, 3.
Pekin Trench, 74, 78.
Petit Vimy, 17.
Picardy, 14.
Pietre, 20, 23, 77, 91.
Pit 8, 43.
Poland, 7, 71.
Politics, 3.
Pont à Vendin, 5, 19, 21, 57, 60, 81.
Port Arthur, 11, 91.
Prince's Road, 68.
Prussian Guard, 47.
Puits 13 bis, 55, 56, 57, 58, 80, 83.
Puits 14 bis, 43, 45, 46, 47, 53, 84, 86, 94.

Q
Quadrilateral, 69, 70.
Quarries, 29, 41, 42, 43, 45, 47, 48, 55, 59, 61, 62, 79, 81, 82, 83, 86, 94.
Quarry Trench, 18, 19, 86.

R
Railway Redoubt, 18.
Regiments, German :
  5, 10, 60.
  14th, 15.
  15th, 10, 92.
  16th, 30, 92.
  21st, 30.
  55th, 10, 92.
  56th, 92.
  77th, 92.
  91st, 92.
  104th, 69.
  117th, 15.
  Guard Reserve, 25.
Reims, 3, 14, 21, 63, 93.
Richebourg d'Avoué, 91.
Roubaix, 4, 7, 8, 66.
Rouges Bancs, 6, 8, 65.
Rue des Cailloux, 68, 69, 92.
Rue du Marais, 6, 8, 11, 64, 67, 92.
Rue d'Ouvert, 11, 69, 92.
Rumania, 3.
Russia, 3, 9, 88.
Russians, 6, 7, 10, 12, 14, 21, 22, 71.

S
St. Elie, 26, 81, 82.
St. Elie Avenue, 19.
St. Nazaire, 17.
St. Quentin, 93.
Salonika, 14, 21, 72.
Saxon, 70.
Scarpe, River, 17.
Scheldt, River, 3, 43, 93.
School House, 70.
Secretary of State for War, 10.
Sedan, 21, 73, 93.
Serbia, 88.
Shells, 3, 11, 13.
Slag Alley, 18.
Smoke, 15.
Soissons, 14, 21, 93.
Somain, 73.
Somme, River, 93.
Souchez, 8, 10, 13, 17, 42, 43, 46, 48, 81.
South Breastwork, 37, 38, 70, 71.
Stafford Corner, 69.
Submarine, 6.
Suvla, 14.

T
Tarnow, 4, 63.
Thelus, 17.
Tournai, 7, 8, 21, 23, 66, 72.
Tortoise Redoubt, 76, 77.
Tower Bridge, 21.
Training, 10.
Triple Alliance, 9.
Turks, 21.

V
Valenciennes, 6, 15, 21, 23, 72, 73, 93.
Vendin le Vieil, 94.
Verdun, 14, 21, 63, 93.
Vermelles, 4, 18, 19, 20, 24, 25, 26, 42, 44, 45, 54, 74, 79, 81, 83, 84, 86, 87, 94.
Ver Touquet, 64.
Ville-sur-Tourne, 6.
Vimy, 4, 5, 7, 8, 9, 10, 17, 43, 46, 58, 60, 66, 86, 93.
Violaines, 9, 11, 36, 70, 91, 92.
Vistula, 14, 71.
Von Spee, 6.
Vouziers, 93.

W
Wallers, 73.
Welch Regiment, 83.
Welch Fusiliers, Royal, 68.
Westende, 23.
Wingles, 57, 94.
Wire, 10, 12, 34, 45, 74.

Y
Ypres, 1, 3, 7, 9, 12, 14, 21, 59, 63, 72, 77, 93.

Printed in Great Britain
by Amazon

50136973R10063